See Through the Scriptures®

Third Edition

Harry Wendt

CROSSWAYS INTERNATIONAL
Minneapolis, MN

See Through the Scriptures®
was developed and written by
Dr. Harry Wendt, Minneapolis, MN, USA
Illustrations by
Knarelle Beard, Adelaide, SA, Australia

See Through the Scriptures®
is published and distributed by
CROSSWAYS INTERNATIONAL
7930 Computer Avenue South
Minneapolis, MN 55435, USA
www.crossways.org

ISBN 1-891245-08-2

Third Edition

Foreword

Al-Azhar University in Cairo, Egypt, has about 21,000 students. All applicants seeking admission to the university are required to be able to recite the Koran, the Muslim Scriptures, from memory. The Koran is about two-thirds the length of the Old Testament. Three days are required to recite it. Unfortunately, few Christians read their Scriptures regularly in detail, and few feel the need to memorize anything beyond the few verses they learned as children.

Though not every Christian can go to seminary or Bible college, every Christian should be a life-long student of the Bible. However, it is not enough to exhort Christians to *read* the Bible; they must be *equipped to read it with understanding*. More people would read the Bible if they had access to some hands-on training.

See Through the Scriptures has been produced to provide hands-on training. It is designed to serve as a tool to convince people that:

We need to *read* the Bible.

We can *understand* the Bible's message.

We can *explain* that message to others.

If people are to make sense out of the Bible, three things are important:

We need to know the biblical story-line *(narrative analysis)*.

We need to know the themes that weave their way through that story-line *(narrative theology)*.

We need to see what Jesus does with the biblical story-line and its themes *(systematization of Jesus' teachings)*.

When Jesus explained to the two disciples on the way to Emmaus the things about Himself (Luke 24:13–35), He did so on the basis of "Moses and all the prophets," namely: Genesis, Exodus, Leviticus, Numbers, Deuteronomy, Joshua, Judges, 1 and 2 Samuel, 1 and 2 Kings, Isaiah, Jeremiah, Ezekiel, and Hosea through Malachi. This manual will use a similar method to explain Jesus' ministry and mission.

We pray that **See Through the Scriptures** will whet many people's appetites to become biblical bloodhounds—people who will saturate themselves in the Scriptures and ask constantly, "What does this mean? What is it saying to me and to God's people?"

Dr. Harry Wendt
Minneapolis, MN

Note: Many of the illustrations in **See Through the Scriptures** make use of a symbol for God. This symbol consists of a circle with four arrows protruding from it. God is *one* (***one*** circle), *without beginning or end* (as a ***circle***). God always acts in *love* (***arrows***), and that love always goes *out* from God (the arrows point ***outward***).

Contents

ILLUSTRATION
1

Where Do You Live?

When asked, "Where do you live?" we usually think of:

- ▲ The name of our street and the number of our house
- ▲ The name of the city or town in which we live
- ▲ The state and country in which these are located

Upper section of **ILLUSTRATION 1**

This picture, based on photographic images from NASA, invites us to broaden our thinking. It shows the majestic spiral galaxy NGC 4414, about 60 million light-years from Planet Earth. A light-year is the distance light travels in a year—approximately six trillion miles (9.6 trillion kilometers). The universe contains tens of billions of such galaxies, each containing hundreds of billions of stars, making the universe so big that its vastness is impossible to comprehend.

If the Milky Way galaxy, in which our solar system is located, could be seen from a distance, it would look like the galaxy depicted—a giant pinwheel about 100,000 light-years in diameter. It spins around its axis once every 200 million years. The Milky Way galaxy contains about 100 billion stars. To count them at the rate of one per second would take about 3,000 years.

Lower section of **ILLUSTRATION 1**

This depicts the immediate solar system in which Planet Earth is located. Though the distances between the planets are obviously not to scale, the relative dimensions of the sun and the planets are. To the left is the side of the sun. Flames, thousands of miles long, leap continually from the surface along the sun's magnetic field. The temperature on the surface of the sun is about 6,000° C.

To the right of the sun are the nine planets which we think of as our "local solar system." If the sun were reduced to the size of a beach ball 24 inches (60 centimeters) in diameter, the planets could be represented as follows:

Mercury: a grain of mustard seed 164 feet (50 meters) away

Venus: a pea 284 feet (87 meters) away

Earth: a pea 430 feet (131 meters) away, with the moon a grain of mustard seed 13 feet (4 meters) out from the earth.

Mars: a raisin 654 feet (200 meters) away

Jupiter: an orange half a mile (804 meters) away

Saturn: a tangerine four-fifths of a mile (1.3 kilometers) away

Uranus: a plum just over a mile (1.6 kilometers) away

Neptune: a plum over two miles (3.2 kilometers) away

Pluto: a pinhead about three miles (4.8 kilometers) away

Our solar system is small when compared with other stars and planets. If the sun were placed at the center of Betelgeuse, a bright red star in the constellation Orion, both Earth and Mars would move around the sun as they do at present distances, and remain within Betelgeuse—which is 431 million miles (694 million kilometers) in diameter. Antares, a double and variable star in the constellation Scorpius, and the brightest star in the southern sky, is 522 million miles (840 million kilometers) in diameter.

In the mid-nineteenth century, Dr. Charles Eliot, the president of Harvard University, wrote:

> *If you say "there is no God," I can only ask how you—a speck of mortal living for a moment of time on an atom of an earth in plain sight of an infinite universe full of incredible beauty, wonder and design—can so confidently hold so improbable a view.*

ILLUSTRATION 2

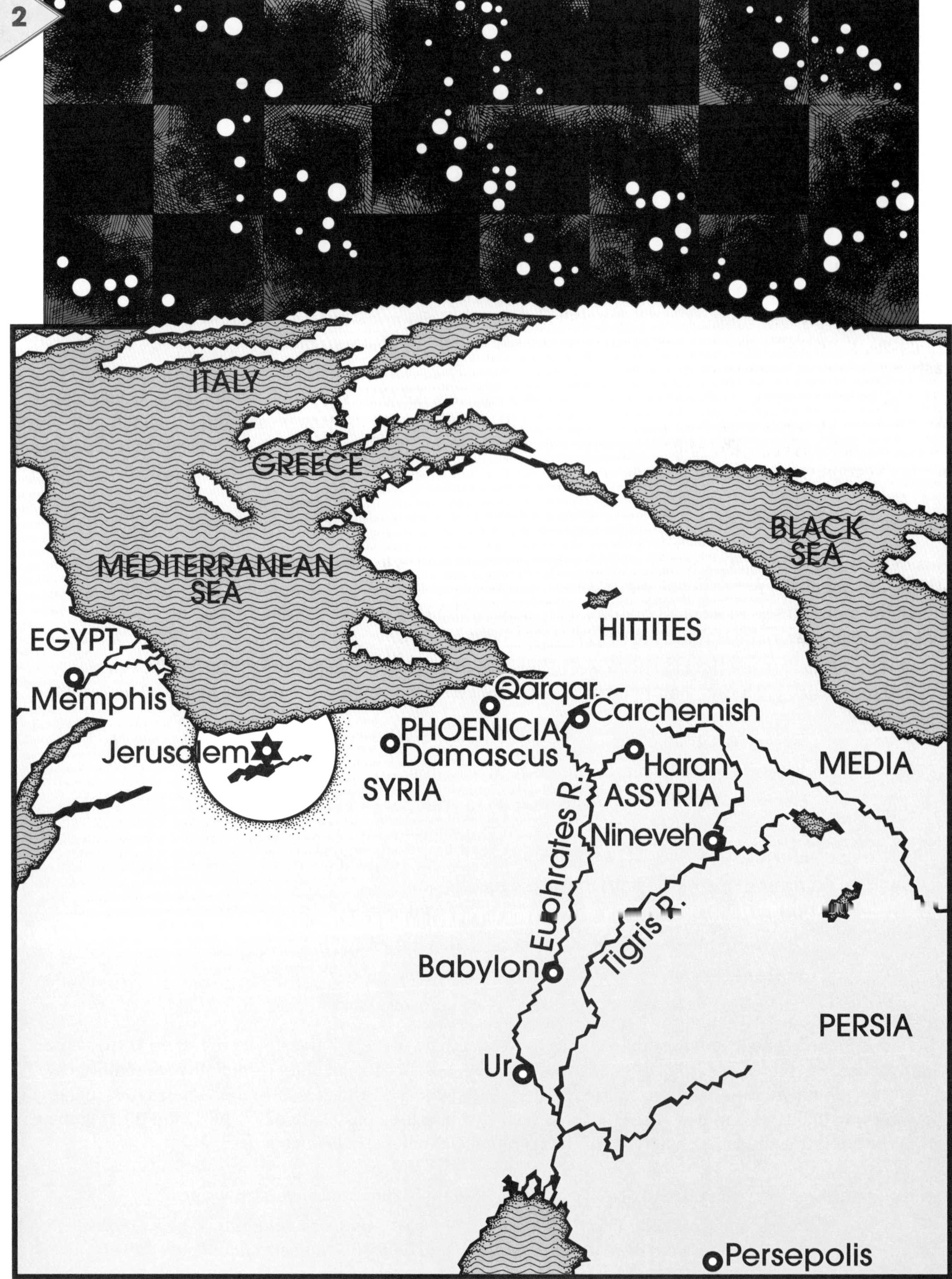

ILLUSTRATION

2

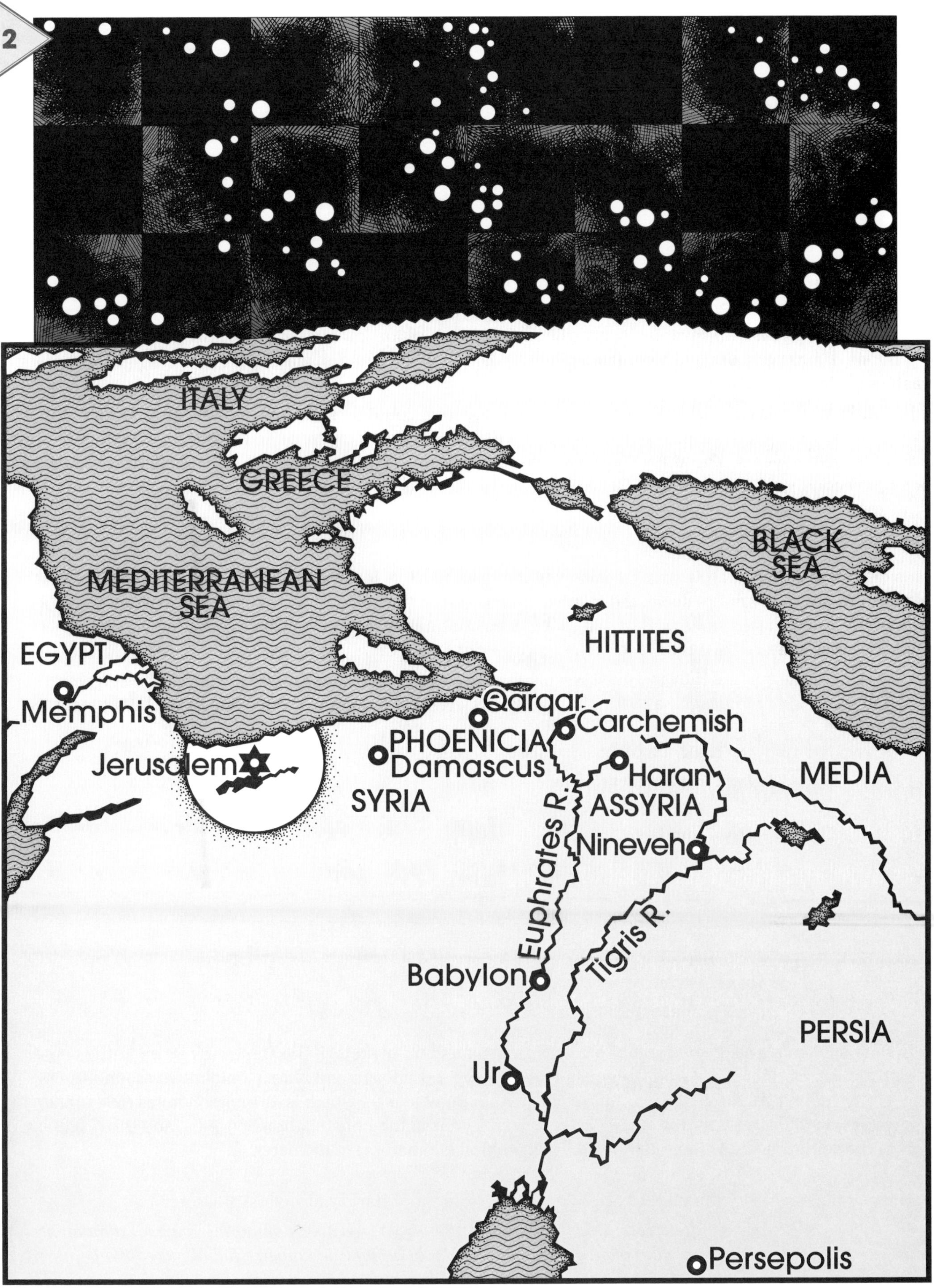

ITALY
GREECE
MEDITERRANEAN SEA
BLACK SEA
HITTITES
EGYPT
Memphis
Qarqar
Carchemish
PHOENICIA
Damascus
Jerusalem
SYRIA
Haran
MEDIA
ASSYRIA
Nineveh
Euphrates R.
Tigris R.
Babylon
PERSIA
Ur
Persepolis

Where Do You Live?

When asked, "Where do you live?" we usually think of:

- The name of our street and the number of our house
- The name of the city or town in which we live
- The state and country in which these are located

Upper section of **ILLUSTRATION 1**

This picture, based on photographic images from NASA, invites us to broaden our thinking. It shows the majestic spiral galaxy NGC 4414, about 60 million light-years from Planet Earth. A light-year is the distance light travels in a year—approximately six trillion miles (9.6 trillion kilometers). The universe contains tens of billions of such galaxies, each containing hundreds of billions of stars, making the universe so big that its vastness is impossible to comprehend.

If the Milky Way galaxy, in which our solar system is located, could be seen from a distance, it would look like the galaxy depicted—a giant pinwheel about 100,000 light-years in diameter. It spins around its axis once every 200 million years. The Milky Way galaxy contains about 100 billion stars. To count them at the rate of one per second would take about 3,000 years.

Lower section of **ILLUSTRATION 1**

This depicts the immediate solar system in which Planet Earth is located. Though the distances between the planets are obviously not to scale, the relative dimensions of the sun and the planets are. To the left is the side of the sun. Flames, thousands of miles long, leap continually from the surface along the sun's magnetic field. The temperature on the surface of the sun is about 6,000° C.

To the right of the sun are the nine planets which we think of as our "local solar system." If the sun were reduced to the size of a beach ball 24 inches (60 centimeters) in diameter, the planets could be represented as follows:

Mercury: a grain of mustard seed 164 feet (50 meters) away

Venus: a pea 284 feet (87 meters) away

Earth: a pea 430 feet (131 meters) away, with the moon a grain of mustard seed 13 feet (4 meters) out from the earth.

Mars: a raisin 654 feet (200 meters) away

Jupiter: an orange half a mile (804 meters) away

Saturn: a tangerine four-fifths of a mile (1.3 kilometers) away

Uranus: a plum just over a mile (1.6 kilometers) away

Neptune: a plum over two miles (3.2 kilometers) away

Pluto: a pinhead about three miles (4.8 kilometers) away

Our solar system is small when compared with other stars and planets. If the sun were placed at the center of Betelgeuse, a bright red star in the constellation Orion, both Earth and Mars would move around the sun as they do at present distances, and remain within Betelgeuse—which is 431 million miles (694 million kilometers) in diameter. Antares, a double and variable star in the constellation Scorpius, and the brightest star in the southern sky, is 522 million miles (840 million kilometers) in diameter.

In the mid-nineteenth century, Dr. Charles Eliot, the president of Harvard University, wrote:

> *If you say "there is no God," I can only ask how you—a speck of mortal living for a moment of time on an atom of an earth in plain sight of an infinite universe full of incredible beauty, wonder and design—can so confidently hold so improbable a view.*

The Book that is a Library

The Greek word from which the English word "Bible" is derived means "book." However, the Bible is really a ***library of books*** written by numerous authors over many hundreds of years.

ILLUSTRATION 3 depicts three shelves of books.

- The ***first*** contains the books that make up the **Hebrew Scriptures**, and shows the manner in which they are grouped.
- The ***second*** contains the **Old Testament** books in Bibles traditionally used by Protestants, and the order in which they are placed in those Bibles. The Roman Catholic Church adds a number of books to the Old Testament; these are generally referred to as the *Apocryphal* or *Deuterocanonical* books. Many Bibles used by Protestants also contain these books. The Apocryphal books contain information that throws light on the history and faith of God's people in the period between the Testaments.
- The ***third*** contains the **New Testament** books used by Protestants and Roman Catholics.

The Hebrew Bible contains only those Old Testament books used by Protestants. It refers to:

- Genesis through Deuteronomy as the ***Law*** (or *Torah*). The Law depicts the origin of the ancient Israelites and defines their mission.
- Joshua, Judges, 1 and 2 Samuel, 1 and 2 Kings as the ***Former Prophets***, and Isaiah, Jeremiah, Ezekiel, and Hosea through Malachi as the ***Latter Prophets*** (or *Nebiim*).
- The ***Former Prophets*** describe how the Israelites forsook their God-given mission, worshiped other gods and eventually were taken into exile to Assyria and Babylon.
- The ***Latter Prophets*** consist of the writings of Israel's ancient prophets who warned the people that they were ignoring God's goodness and will for their lives, and that tragedy would overtake them if they did not repent and return to the God of their fathers.
- The rest of the books are known as the ***Writings*** (or *Ketubim*). The Writings, among other things, describe how the exiles who returned from Babylon reestablished themselves and their Jerusalem-based worship system in the "Promised Land."

The Jewish religious community refers to its Bible as ***TaNaK***, a word made up of the first letters in ***T****orah*, ***N****ebiim*, and ***K****etubim*. Christian scholars generally consider the Jewish division of the Old Testament more appropriate.

The point of departure between the Jewish faith and Christianity has to do with the person of Jesus of Nazareth. Was He the promised Messiah? Judaism says "No." Christianity says "Yes."

- ***Jews*** insist that Jesus was not the Messiah because the Messiah of Jewish expectation would be a great teacher and leader who would, among other things, make *Jerusalem* the political, moral, and spiritual capital of the world.
- ***Christians*** believe that the pivotal event in biblical history is the life, sacrificial death, and resurrection of Jesus the Messiah, the incarnate Son of God, for all humanity.

ILLUSTRATION 4

Putting the Pieces Together

At the *bottom* of **ILLUSTRATION 4** is a ***face*** with a ***question mark*** above it. Let's name the person Sylvester. The question mark above his head indicates that he is asking many questions about the Christian faith. He sees the Christian faith and everything related to it as one big puzzle (***black lines indicating jigsaw puzzle***). He finds it hard to fit all the bits and pieces together. He is asking:

 ***Bible:*** "How can I make sense out of the Bible? I can't fit it all together."

 ***Person wearing clerical collar:*** "I really want to serve God full-time with my life. Must I become a pastor or priest to do that?"

 ***Faces and music:*** "If I can't serve God full-time as a clergy-person, can I perhaps serve God part-time by singing in a church choir?"

 ***Law tablets:*** "The commandments were given so long ago. Do they still apply to me and my life today?"

 ***Angel on cloud:*** "What is an angel? Are there bad ones as well as good ones?"

 ***Dollar sign on envelope:*** "Christians give money to their church. Why? How much?"

 ***Church building:*** "There are many different church denominations. Which is right?"

 ***Gravestone:*** "Christian preachers and people talk a lot about death. Why do we die? Can we know for sure what happens to us after death?"

Some who come into contact with the Christian faith feel like jugglers trying to deal with too many things at once. They struggle to fit the Bible's many details together.

In the pages that follow, the pieces of the puzzle will be fitted together to make a complete picture. The picture that finally emerges is of Jesus, the Messiah—who proclaimed, displayed, and established the eternal Kingdom of God. (For a "sneak preview," see **ILLUSTRATION 36** and **ILLUSTRATION 42**.)

Still today, Jesus gathers people into His Kingdom in forgiving grace and calls them to follow Him in sacrificial servanthood.

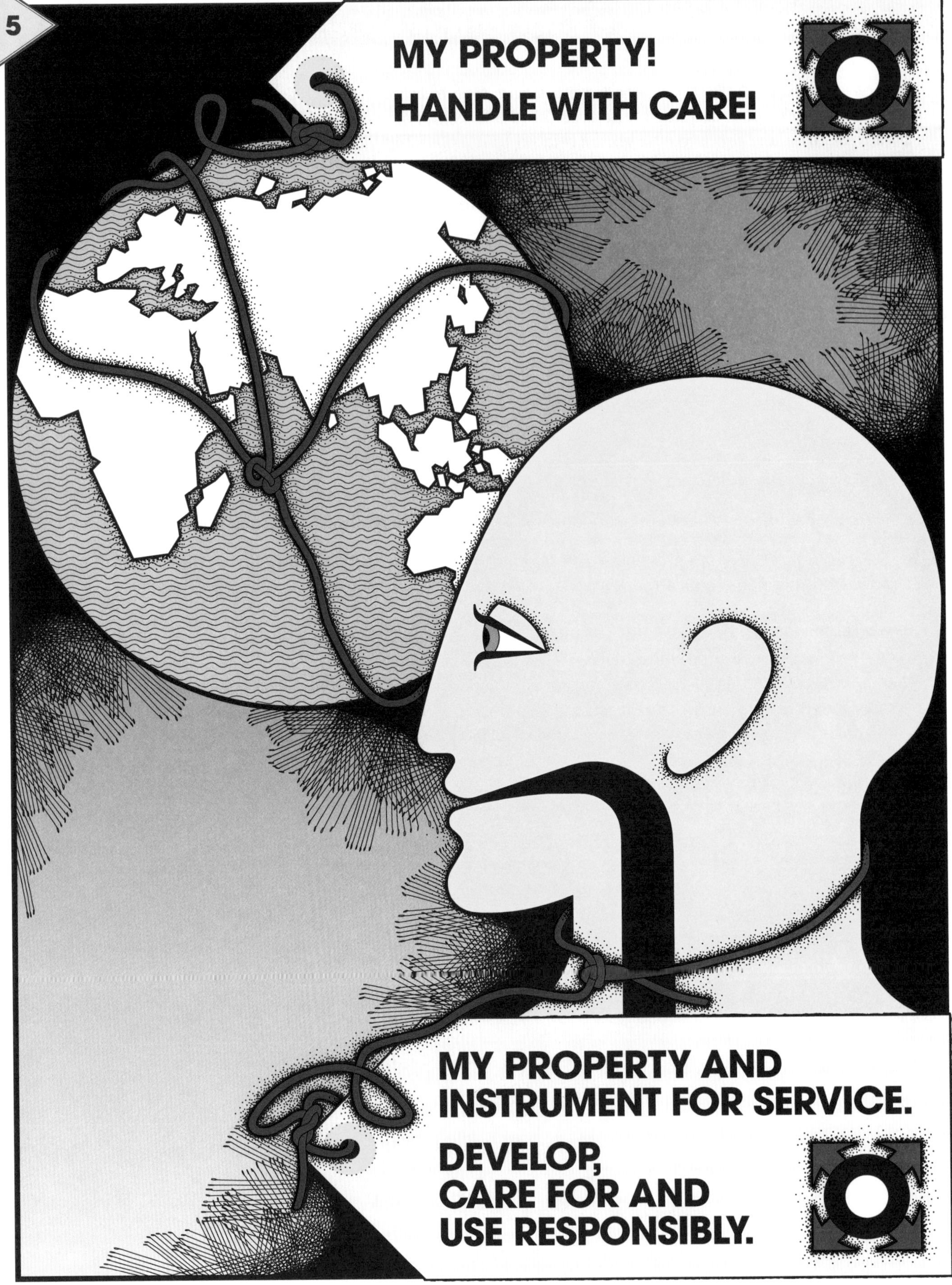
MY PROPERTY!
HANDLE WITH CARE!
MY PROPERTY AND
INSTRUMENT FOR SERVICE.
DEVELOP,
CARE FOR AND
USE RESPONSIBLY.

Empires Come, Empires Go!

Some think that the people in the Bible lived in cozy comfort, insulated from the history of surrounding nations, and devoted themselves wholeheartedly to the worship and service of God. Not so! They lived among superpowers that were constantly at war with each other, and they worshiped a variety of gods.

ILLUSTRATION 2 depicts what might be termed "an astronaut's view" of the ***Mediterranean*** world in which the biblical narrative unfolds, and the major players in that narrative. (The name *Mediterranean* is derived from two Latin words that mean "in the middle of land.") The land of *Canaan* (***white circle***) is located at "center stage." The *Israelites* who settled in Canaan were the descendants of Abraham, Isaac, and Jacob (the "patriarchs"). David captured ***Jerusalem*** and made it his capital, 2 Samuel 5:6–10.

There were usually tensions and unhappy relations between the Israelites and ***Syria***. Good relations prevailed between the Israelites and ***Phoenicians***. The Phoenicians were a sea-faring people (the Israelites were not) who played an important role in international trading ventures. The Israelites needed access to their sea-faring skills and services.

The region between the ***Tigris*** and ***Euphrates*** Rivers was known as *Mesopotamia*—a name derived from two Greek words meaning "between the rivers."

The ***Assyrians***, ***Babylonians***, and ***Persians*** established successive empires in Mesopotamia. The Babylonians conquered Assyrian ***Nineveh*** in 612 B.C. Cyrus the Persian gained control of ***Media*** in 550 B.C., and conquered ***Babylon*** in 539 B.C. The ***Greeks*** under Alexander the Great ravaged ***Persepolis***, a major Persian capital city, in 330 B.C. In 40–37 B.C., the *Parthians* (not shown; to the northeast of Media) helped Antigonus, a descendant of the Jewish rulers (165–63), gain control of Judea and Jerusalem—and block Rome's "land bridge" to ***Egypt***.

The ***Hittites***, ***Assyrians***, ***Babylonians***, ***Persians***, ***Greeks,*** and *Romans* consistently cast covetous eyes on ***Egypt***, whose fertile *Nile Valley* was the bread-basket of the ancient Mediterranean world. When these ancient superpowers set out to plunder Egypt's resources, they naturally marched through Canaan along the way. The Mesopotamian nations could not follow a direct route to Egypt, but had to travel "between the rivers" and down the Mediterranean coast to ensure access to food and water.

The Egyptians were aware of the ambitions and needs of their northern neighbors. To discourage invasions by them, the Egyptians built a series of fortresses along the Mediterranean coast. The northernmost of these was located at ***Carchemish***—which enabled the Egyptians to block the advance of Mesopotamian nations and discourage the empire-building dreams of southern European powers.

Because nations believed that their gods led them into battle and gave them their victories, they usually placed symbols of the gods of conquered nations in their shrines (1 Samuel 5:1,2), and symbols of their gods in the shrines of those they conquered. In 2 Kings 23:4,5 the references to "the host of heaven" and "the sun, the moon, the constellations, and all the host of the heavens" in the Jerusalem Temple are to Assyrian astral deities.

On occasion, God declared that He would use other nations, such as Assyria and Babylon, to discipline His own rebellious people; see Isaiah 10:5, Jeremiah 27:6.

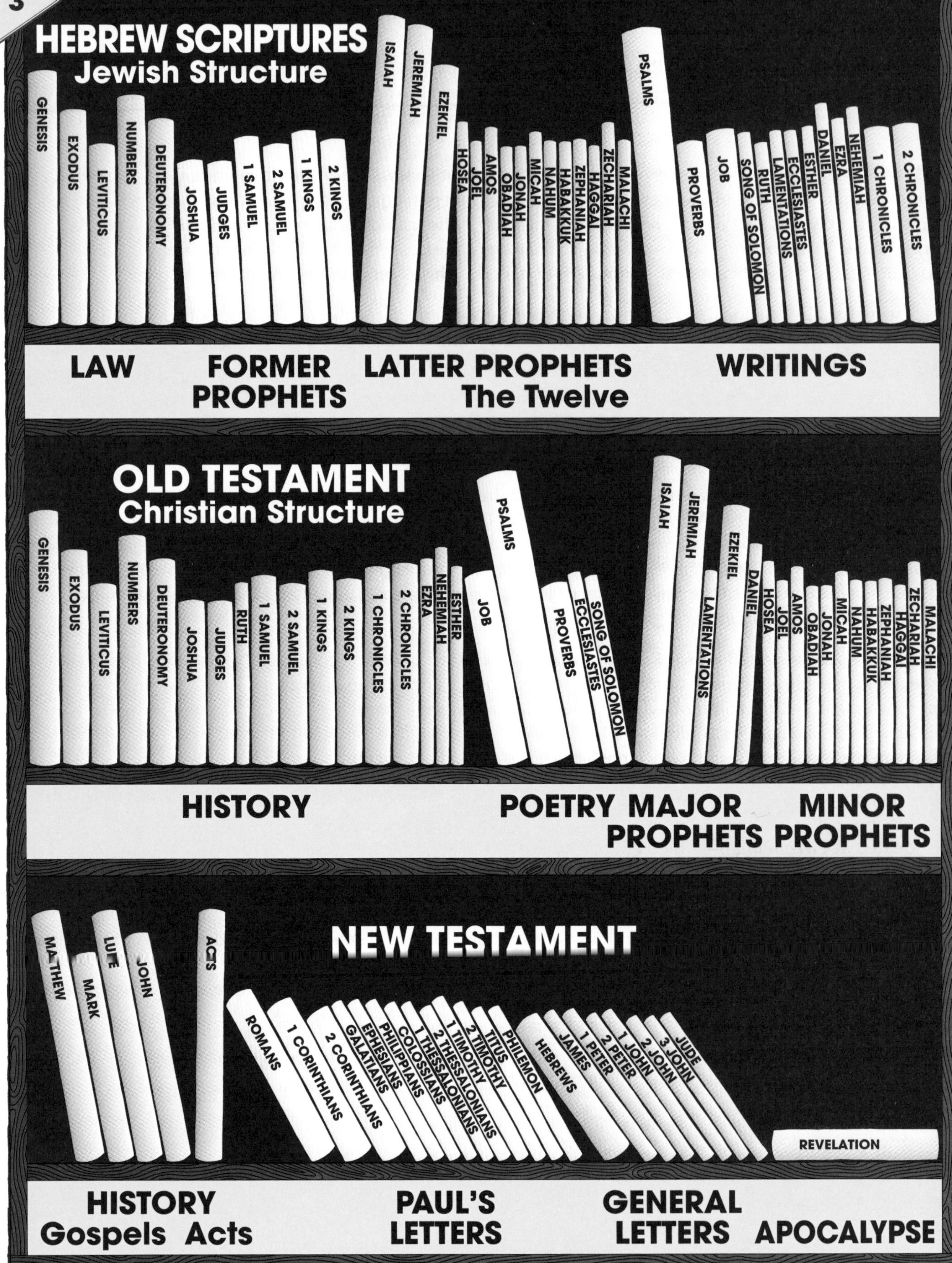
ILLUSTRATION
3
HEBREW SCRIPTURES
Jewish Structure
GENESIS
EXODUS
LEVITICUS
NUMBERS
DEUTERONOMY
JOSHUA
JUDGES
1 SAMUEL
2 SAMUEL
1 KINGS
2 KINGS
ISAIAH
JEREMIAH
EZEKIEL
HOSEA
JOEL
AMOS
OBADIAH
JONAH
MICAH
NAHUM
HABAKKUK
ZEPHANIAH
HAGGAI
ZECHARIAH
MALACHI
PSALMS
PROVERBS
JOB
SONG OF SOLOMON
RUTH
LAMENTATIONS
ECCLESIASTES
ESTHER
DANIEL
EZRA
NEHEMIAH
1 CHRONICLES
2 CHRONICLES
LAW
FORMER PROPHETS
LATTER PROPHETS
The Twelve
WRITINGS
OLD TESTAMENT
Christian Structure
GENESIS
EXODUS
LEVITICUS
NUMBERS
DEUTERONOMY
JOSHUA
JUDGES
RUTH
1 SAMUEL
2 SAMUEL
1 KINGS
2 KINGS
1 CHRONICLES
2 CHRONICLES
EZRA
NEHEMIAH
ESTHER
JOB
PSALMS
PROVERBS
ECCLESIASTES
SONG OF SOLOMON
ISAIAH
JEREMIAH
LAMENTATIONS
EZEKIEL
DANIEL
HOSEA
JOEL
AMOS
OBADIAH
JONAH
MICAH
NAHUM
HABAKKUK
ZEPHANIAH
HAGGAI
ZECHARIAH
MALACHI
HISTORY
POETRY
MAJOR PROPHETS
MINOR PROPHETS
NEW TESTAMENT
MATHEW
MARK
LUKE
JOHN
ACTS
ROMANS
1 CORINTHIANS
2 CORINTHIANS
GALATIANS
EPHESIANS
PHILIPPIANS
COLOSSIANS
1 THESSALONIANS
2 THESSALONIANS
1 TIMOTHY
2 TIMOTHY
TITUS
PHILEMON
HEBREWS
JAMES
1 PETER
2 PETER
1 JOHN
2 JOHN
3 JOHN
JUDE
REVELATION
HISTORY
Gospels Acts
PAUL'S LETTERS
GENERAL LETTERS
APOCALYPSE

Maker and Owner

ILLUSTRATION 5 shows ***Planet Earth*** and a ***human being***, with ***God's ownership label*** attached to each.

Upper section

- God made and owns the universe, including Planet Earth. Everything belongs to God. We own nothing. God "owns the company." We merely use and manage what God made and owns, and are to do so responsibly.
- There is no such thing as "Christian giving." The real problem is "un-Christian robbing" which thinks "I own, and will give some of what is mine—if I feel like doing so."

Lower section

- God made and owns *all people* on Planet Earth, and is not interested in borders, flags, and skin color.
- God lends us the body and life we traditionally refer to as "ours." In the Parable of the Rich Fool (Luke 12:13–21), Jesus *first* points out that God's land, not the rich man, produced abundantly, and *second*, the rich man's life was merely on loan from God.
- God has endowed us with skills and abilities which we are to view with respect and develop responsibly and wisely. We are to use the body and life God is lending us to glorify God by serving others.
- Our actions toward others are to reflect God's prior actions toward us, 1 John 4:19–21. We do not love that God may love us; we love because God already loves us.
- When we live according to God's will, we find meaning and joy in life and bring meaning and joy to others.

ILLUSTRATION
6

The Original Plan

 **ILLUSTRATION 6** depicts God's original plan for humanity—that all should live together on Planet Earth:

- under God as King (***crown***, and the ***symbol for God***),
- as one united family (***community of people holding hands around Planet Earth***),
- with each person asking, "How can I use life to glorify God and serve those around me?" (***servant figures***, ***arrows from each to God and neighbor***, ***law codes***).

 God's plan was that there would be harmony:

- among all people,
- between the sexes (***man and woman serving God and each other*** (*upper section*), and ***holding hands*** (*bottom border; man has yellow buttons on jacket, woman has pink nails*),
- among everyone in different positions and situations in society.

 God says to each of us:

Seek under My grace and power
  to become more and more what I want you to be,
so that I can use you more effectively
  to help others become more and more
    what I want them to be.

 In today's fallen and sinful world, we are to serve others as God wants us to serve them—not as they might want us to serve them, nor as we might want to serve them. God writes the agenda. Each of us is to become more Christlike, and help others become more Christlike.

 Unity would prevail among people if every person on Planet Earth asked one question:

"How can I use life to glorify God and serve others?"

 The following two statements define the **mission of the Church**:

God has made known to us in all wisdom and insight the mystery of His will, which He set forth in Christ, as a plan for the fulness of time, to unite all things in Him, things in heaven and things on earth. (Ephesians 1:9,10, RSV translation)

The mission of the Church is to restore all people to unity with God and each other, in Christ. (Anglican Catechism, *The Book of Common Prayer*, p. 855).

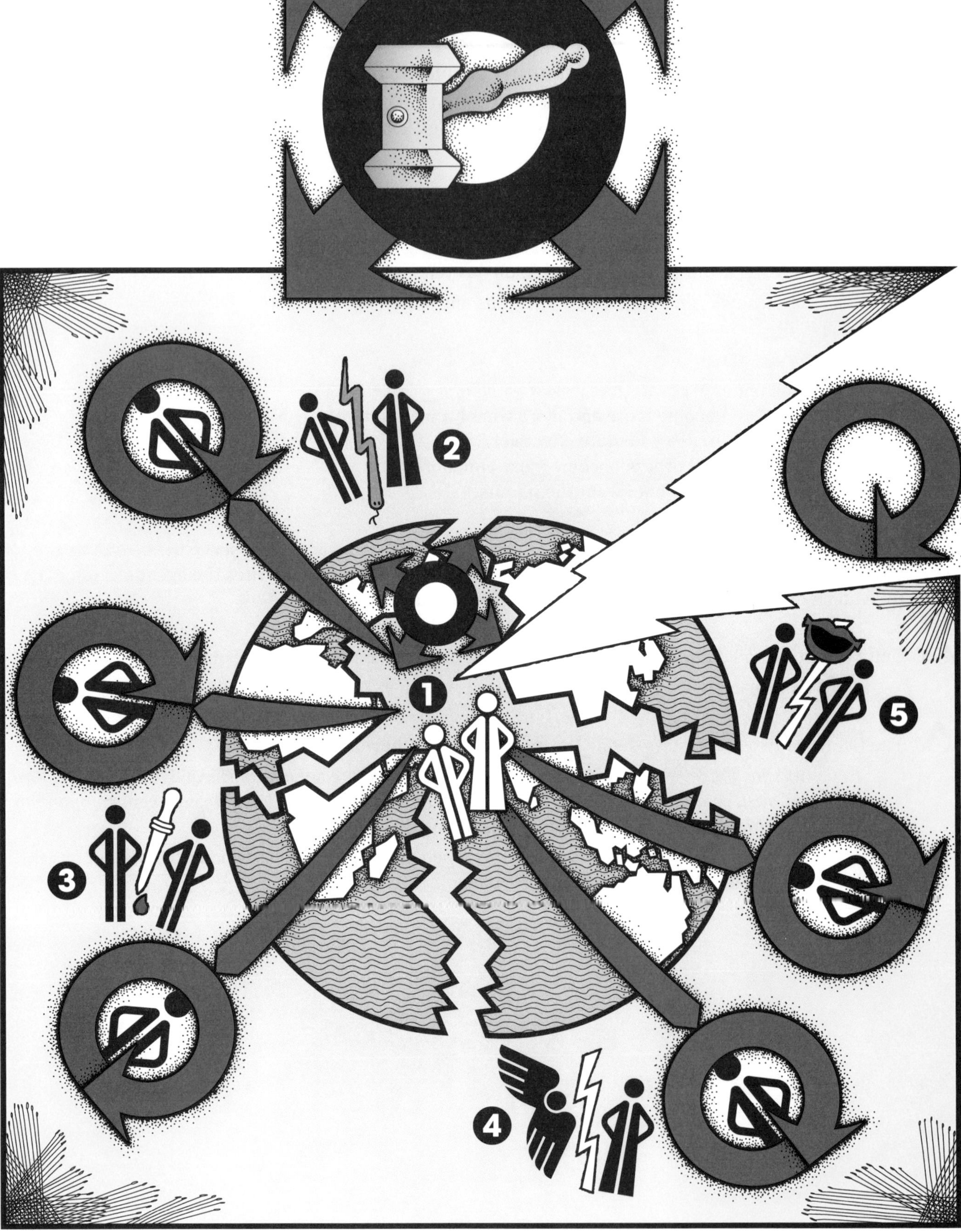
1
2
3
4
5

The Plan Destroyed

The symbols used in this illustration occur in many that follow.

ILLUSTRATION 7 shows the power of sin (***circular arrow***, *center right*) breaking in and destroying God's original plan.

Sin makes people prisoners to self, to their own whims and will (***persons locked in circles***).

Sin tore God's good creation apart at all levels. It broke the relationship between:

1. God and humanity.
2. Man and woman, male and female, Genesis 2,3. (Note the ***dividing serpent***.)
3. Brother and brother, Genesis 4. Cain killed Abel (***knife***, ***drop of blood***).
4. The heavenly and the earthly, Genesis 6:1–4. Divine beings called the "sons of God" (***winged creatures***—Job 1:6, 2:1, 38:7) were sexually intimate with women on earth.
5. Nation and nation, Genesis 11. The building of the tower of Babel resulted in the confusion of languages (***mouth***) and the fragmenting and scattering of humanity across the world.

Sin has brought humanity under God's judgment (***gavel*** on ***symbol for God***).

The result? Issues of race and sex shatter relationships. Concern for the well-being of others has been replaced by the spirit of individualism. People now want to live to serve their own egos, whims, appetites, and ambitions. People eye one another suspiciously.

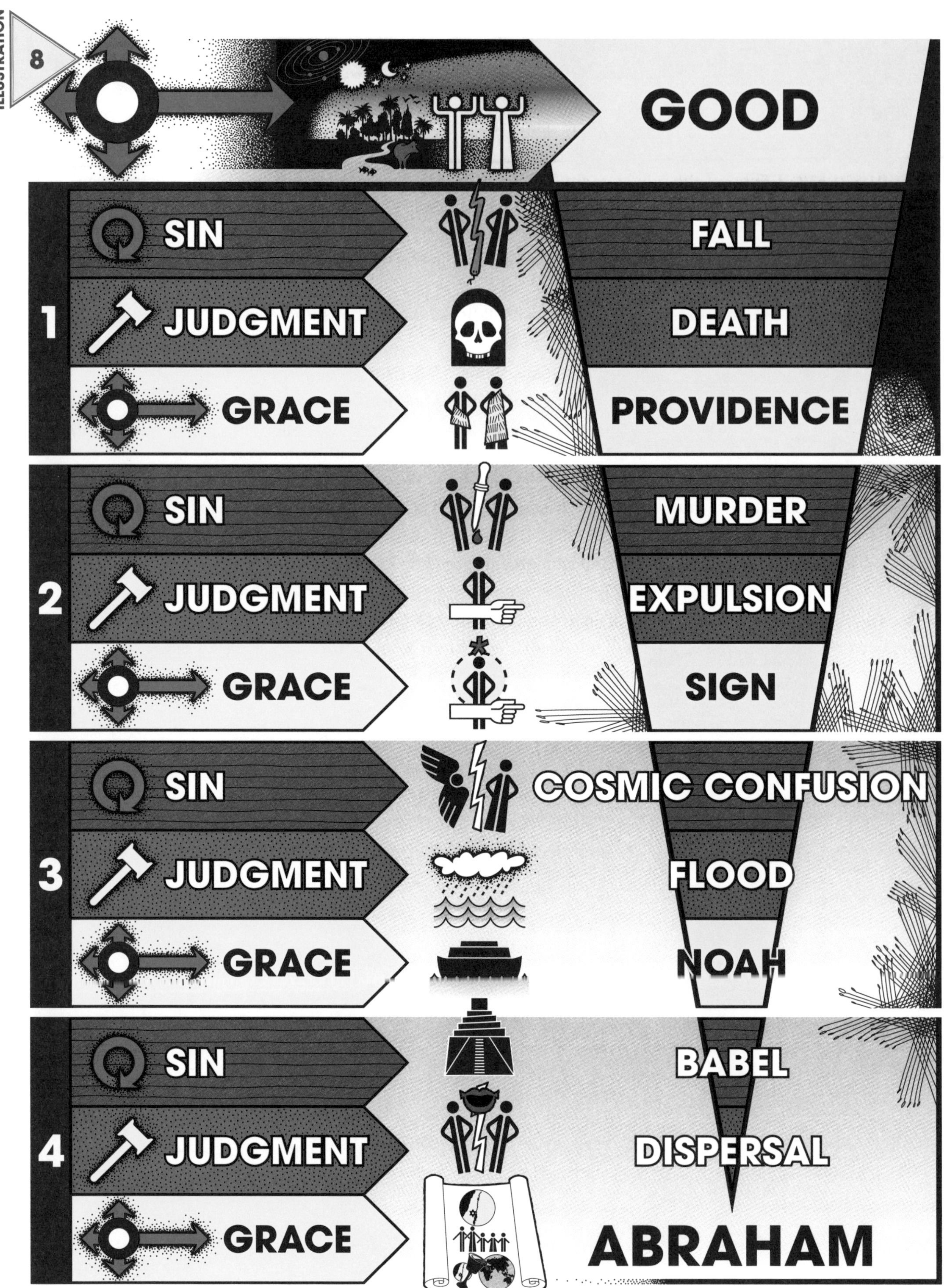
ILLUSTRATION
8
GOOD
SIN
FALL
1
JUDGMENT
DEATH
GRACE
PROVIDENCE
SIN
MURDER
2
JUDGMENT
EXPULSION
GRACE
SIGN
SIN
COSMIC CONFUSION
3
JUDGMENT
FLOOD
GRACE
NOAH
SIN
BABEL
4
JUDGMENT
DISPERSAL
GRACE
ABRAHAM

From Adam to Abraham

The Bible refers to Abraham for the first time in Genesis 11:26; he is the first of the so-called "chosen people." The first eleven chapters of the Bible outline what happened *before* Abraham's call. The rest of its contents describe what happened *after* his call. Genesis 1–11 defines *God's purpose* in calling Abraham and in forming from him a people eventually referred to as the Israelites, Genesis 32:28.

SIN-JUDGMENT-GRACE

Genesis 1 declares that ***God***, who is ***good***, made a ***good creation*** (**ILLUSTRATION 8**, *top segment*). The first parents were to praise and serve God, and serve each other. Key themes run through the four major narratives that follow in Genesis 2–11, with ***God's grace*** being the key theme throughout. Points 1–4 below refer to the numbers in the illustration.

 ***Genesis 2–3***

- **SIN:** Adam and Eve disobey God (***serpent between persons in posture of indifference***).
- **JUDGMENT:** Their sin brings ***death*** (***gavel*** symbolizing ***judgment***; ***tombstone***).
- **GRACE:** God remains in fellowship with them, and ***clothes them in skins***, 3:21.3:21).

 ***Genesis 4–5***

- **SIN:** Cain kills his brother Abel (***knife***, ***drop of blood***).
- **JUDGMENT:** God banishes Cain from His presence (***pointing hand across Cain—"Depart!"***).
- **GRACE:** The Lord puts a protective mark on Cain, 4:15 (***mark***; ***circle around Cain***).

 ***Genesis 6–9***

- **SIN:** Divine beings (***winged creature***) called "the sons of God" (Genesis 6:1; see Job 38:7) are sexually intimate with earthly women.
- **JUDGMENT:** God destroys the face of Planet Earth with a ***flood*** (***cloud***, ***rain***, ***waves***).
- **GRACE:** God preserves ***Noah***, his immediate family, and the animal world (***ark***).

 ***Genesis 10:1–12:3***

- **SIN:** Noah's descendants begin to build a ***tower*** to reach into the heavens "to make a name for themselves" and to prevent being scattered across the face of the earth.
- **JUDGMENT:** God stops the project by confusing their languages (***mouth***) and scattering the people.
- **GRACE:** God calls ***Abraham***, sends him to the land of ***Canaan***, promises that he will have ***many descendants***, and that blessings will flow from them to the nations (***cup***).

The Theology of Genesis 1-11

- Genesis 1–11 tells *who* created the universe, *why* He created it, *how humanity responded* to God's goodness, and *how God responded and responds* to people's sin and rebellion.
- Genesis 1–11 culminates in the call of ***Abraham***, 12:1–3. The God who calls Abraham is none other than the Creator Himself. God is not acting in some new way, but, as always, in ***grace***.
- God had a purpose in calling Abraham: **To work through Abraham and his descendants to restore humanity to God's original plan.** (Compare **ILLUSTRATION 6** with **ILLUSTRATION 7**.)
- The *key word* that weaves its way through the biblical narrative from beginning to end is *grace*!

ILLUSTRATION 9

The Covenant with Abraham

Genesis contains numerous references to what God says He will do for Abraham and achieve through him, Genesis 12:1–3,7; 13:15; 15:18–20; 17:8. The covenant God makes with Abraham, a ***Covenant of Divine Commitment***, is a one-way affair—from God to Abraham (***yellow figure***). In this covenant (depicted in the ***scroll*** in the *lower section* of **ILLUSTRATION 9**), God promises:

- To give Abraham and his descendants the ***land of Canaan***.
- To give Abraham ***offspring*** and build a nation from him.
- To use Abraham and his descendants to bring ***blessings to other nations*** (depicted by ***the contents of a cup over Canaan overflowing across the world***).

The narrative leaves the reader wondering whether God's promises to Abraham will ever be fulfilled. Some of the stories about the first patriarchs, Abraham and Sarah, are full of suspense.

a. Abraham almost loses Sarah to another man, Genesis 12:10–20; 20:1–18.

b. If Lot had chosen Canaan instead of the Jordan Valley, Abraham would have lost his claim to the Promised Land, Genesis 13.

c. Although Abraham and Sarah wait 25 years for the birth of Isaac (Genesis 21), a few years after his birth, God tells Abraham to offer up his son as a sacrifice, Genesis 22. After God spares Abraham the agony of having to sacrifice his son Isaac, God provides Abraham with a ram which he then sacrifices on Mt. Moriah. It is significant that there came a day when David offered sacrifice on this same mountain (2 Sam. 24:18–25)—where Solomon eventually built the Temple, 2 Chron. 3:1.

The behavior of Abraham and Sarah is sometimes questionable:

a. Both Abraham and Sarah suggest alternative plans for obtaining an heir: adoption, 15:1–6; concubinage, ch. 16; 17:18.

b. Both laugh at God and suggest that the idea of the aged Sarah becoming pregnant is ridiculous, 17:17; 18:12. (The name *Isaac* means "laughter.")

At the end of his life, Abraham has one "chosen son" by Sarah and two grandsons by Isaac, Genesis 21 and 25:19–26. All Abraham owns of Canaan is a field and a burial cave bought for 400 shekels of silver, ch. 23. After Sarah's death, he takes another wife and some concubines, and has more children, 25:1–11.

Why did God choose Abraham, and not someone else?

a. God did not call Abraham because he was more righteous than others, deserved God's call, or had great faith or leadership potential. Joshua 24:2 states that at the time of his call, Abraham, like all his contemporaries, was an idolater (***idols***).

b. God called Abraham in grace—nothing else. However, God called him to be the first of a people through whom God would work to put the fragmented human race back together again.

The promise concerning the land of Canaan is sealed in a solemn ceremony. God's presence (symbolized by a ***smoking fire-pot and a flaming torch***) passes between animals that have been cut in two—an action that declares, "May the fate that has overtaken these animals overtake Me if I break My promise to you," Genesis 15:7–21. In the course of this ceremony, God assures Abraham that his descendants will indeed eventually get the land—in 400 years time!

ILLUSTRATION 10

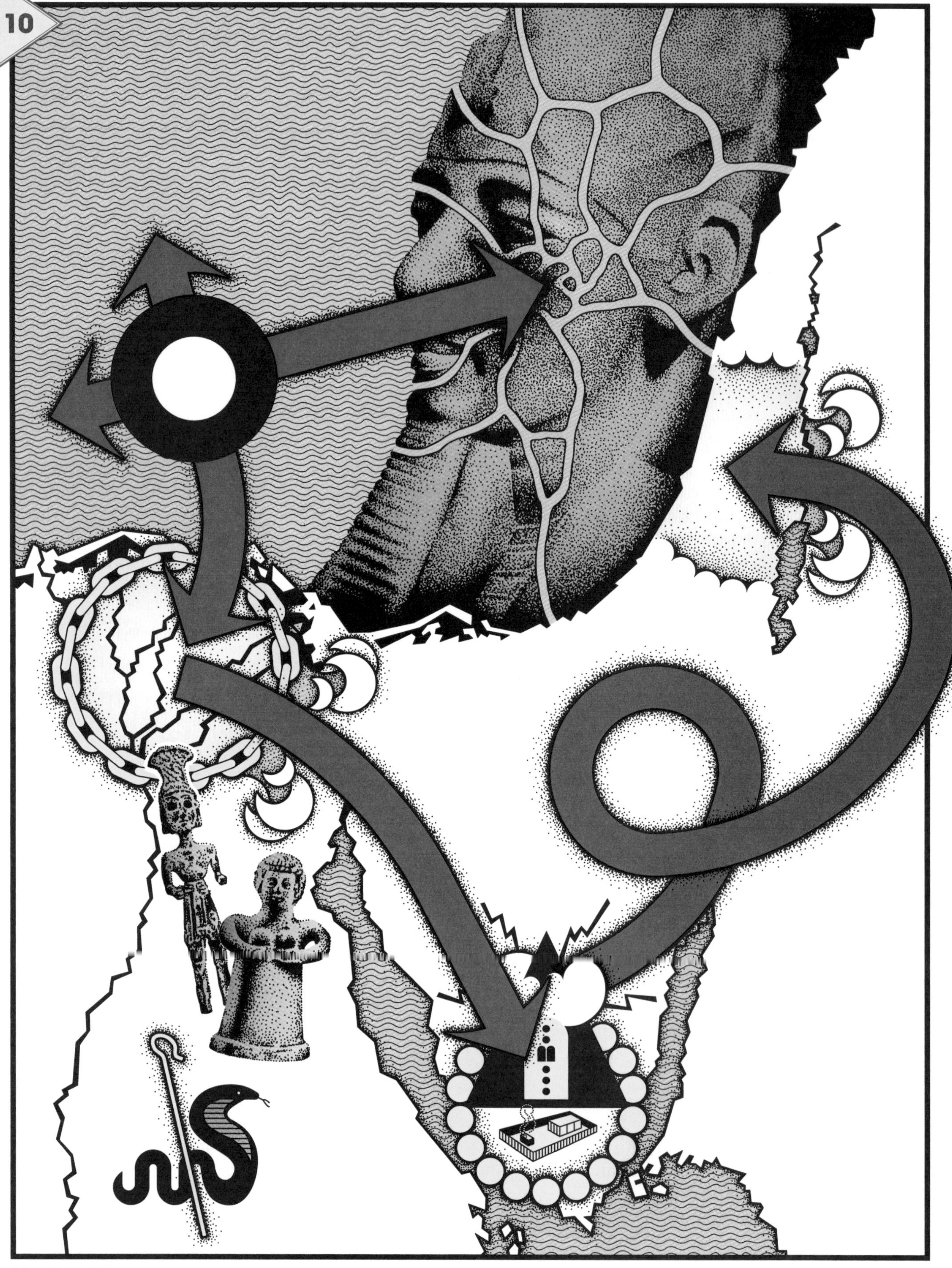

The Exodus from Egypt

Circle of chains around the Nile Delta: The closing chapters of Genesis describe Israel happily settled in Egypt. The opening chapters of Exodus speak of Israel *in slavery in Egypt*.

Arrow from the symbol for God pointing to the pharaoh's broken face: The Egyptian pharaoh is so worried by Israel's increase in numbers that he tries to destroy the nation in two ways: by enslaving the Israelites, and by ordering midwives to kill all their male infants, Exodus ch. 1. God engages in a holy war with the pharaoh, and conquers him.

Staff and serpent: When Israel's leaders, Moses and Aaron, confront the Egyptian magicians, both sides cast rods (important symbols of authority) to the ground which transform into snakes. Aaron's rod-become-serpent swallows the Egyptian rods-become-serpents, Exodus 7:8–13.

Waves, and arrow through chains and waves: In the battle of the plagues that follows, God defeats the pharaoh, leads the Israelites out of Egypt, and then destroys the pharaoh and his army when they pursue Israel through the opening in the sea, Exodus chs. 1–14.

God leads Israel into the wilderness, gathers the people around Him at Mt. Sinai and makes a covenant with them (***covenant symbol on Mt. Sinai***). God summons Moses to come up the mountain and gives him law codes to direct the lives of the people, Exodus 20 (***symbol for law codes on symbol for covenant***). The law codes were guidelines for:

- *Copying God.* The people were to serve each other as God served them.
- *Living in community* (***circle of dots around Mt. Sinai***).
- *Experiencing blessedness and joy*, Deuteronomy 28:1–14.
- *Witnessing.* Other nations, seeing Israel's obedience, would feel moved to inquire about Israel's God, Deuteronomy 4:6–8; see also John 13:34,35. Israel's life in serving community was to reflect how God wanted the first people He made to live; see **ILLUSTRATION 6**.

While Israel remains encamped around Mt. Sinai, God shows His continuing presence at its summit by means of a ***storm cloud***, ***lightning***, fire, and trumpet blasts, Exodus 19. Later, God takes up residence among His people in a portable shrine referred to as both the ***Tabernacle*** (*depicted*, Exodus chs. 25–31, 35–40) and the Tent of Meeting, Exodus 33:7–11.

The people spend nearly a year at Sinai, Exodus 19:1–Numbers 10:11. God then leads them on a 39-year journey ***through the wilderness*** (***looped arrow***).

The narrative that describes Israel's time in the wilderness speaks only of disobedience and rebellion on their part, and mercy and patience on God's part, Numbers 10:11–36:13; Deuteronomy chs. 1–3.

Finally God opens up a way for the people to pass ***through the Jordan River into the Promised Land***, Joshua 3 (***waters of the Jordan opened***).

God did not rescue the Israelites because they worshiped Him while in Egypt; they worshiped ***idols in Egypt***, Joshua 24:14,15, Ezekiel 20:1–8a. Nor did God rescue them because they were obeying His commandments; the commandments were given at Sinai *after the Israelites had left Egypt.* **The key theme throughout is God's grace, goodness, and mercy.**

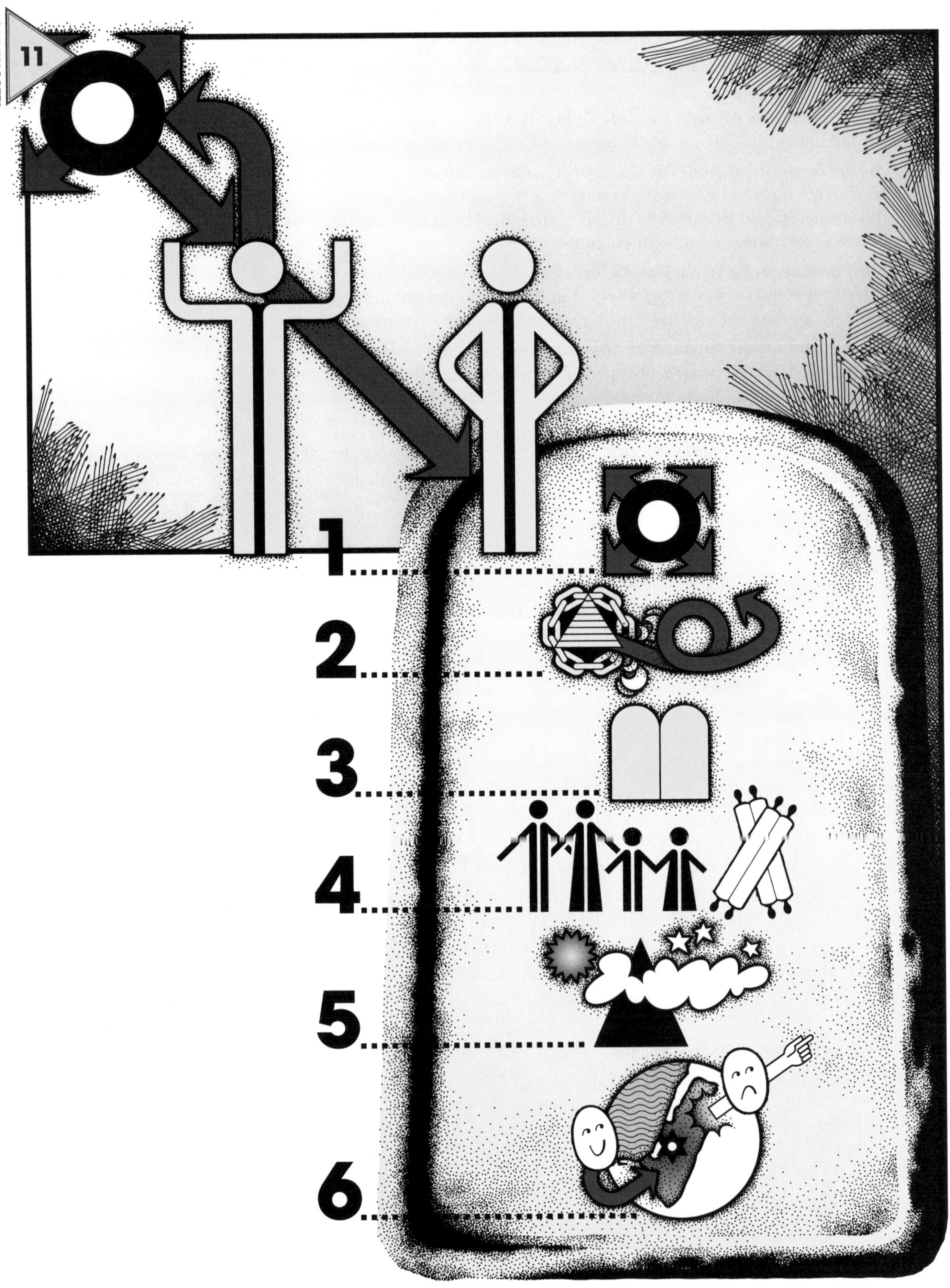
ILLUSTRATION
11
1
2
3
4
5
6

The Covenant at Sinai

ILLUSTRATION 11 outlines the six sections of the covenant God made with Israel at Sinai.

 ***Preamble:*** God tells the people who He is, "I am the Lord your God," Exodus 20:2 (***symbol for God***).

 ***Historical Prologue:*** God tells the people what He has done for them, "...who brought you out of the land of Egypt, out of the house of slavery," Exodus 20:2 (***Egyptian pyramid***, ***arrow through chains and water***, ***circular arrow denoting journey through wilderness and entry into the Promised Land***).

 ***Commandments*** (or ***Stipulations***)***:*** God tells the people what He expects them to do for Him in response, Exodus 20:3–17. The first five books of the Old Testament contain several collections of these stipulations, or law codes.

The people's obedience is not to be an attempt to *affect* a relationship with God; it is to *reflect* the relationship God has established with them. The people are to serve one another as God has served them, Deuteronomy 16:12.

 ***Preservation and rereading:*** The covenant is to be written and stored, read regularly to future generations of Israelites—and obeyed, Exodus 34:23,24; Deuteronomy 31:9–13, 24–26 (***parents with children***, ***scrolls***).

 ***Witnesses:*** Witnesses watch over the covenant to ensure that it is kept, Deuteronomy 30:19, 31:28; Joshua 24:22,27. In non-Israelite covenant forms, the gods are called to serve as witnesses to covenants earthly kings made with each other. In Israel the forces of nature (***mountain***, ***cloud***, ***sun***, ***stars***) and the people themselves serve as witnesses to the covenant God made with the Israelites.

 ***Blessings and Curses:*** If the people take the covenant seriously, all will go well for them (***smiling face***) in Canaan (***arrow pointing to the Promised Land***), Deuteronomy 28:1–14. If they do not, things will go badly for them (***sad face***), and they will lose the land to a foreign power and be taken into exile (***hand pointing to a distant land***), Deuteronomy 28:15–68.

The difference between the covenant with Abraham and the covenant at Sinai was:

- God made a one-way *Covenant of Divine Commitment* with Abraham in which God committed Himself to do certain things for Abraham and his offspring. Israel could negate that covenant by persistently running after other gods, 1 Kings 9:1–9.
- The covenant God made with Israel at Sinai (*Covenant of Human Obligation*) was one in which God, after spelling out who He was and what He had done for His people, outlined the path of obedience they were to walk. Israel could break it—by persistent disobedience, Deuteronomy 8:11–20.

ILLUSTRATION 12

BECAUSE

THEREFORE

Because I—Therefore You

People do not earn acceptance from God by good deeds. They cannot! God never intended that people even try to do this. All such attempts are misguided and contrary to God's will, Romans 3:27,28.

Throughout the Bible, God first tells people who He is and what He has done for them. Only then does God state what He wishes people to do for Him—that they should serve Him by serving others. The sequence is always, "*Because I* (God)—*therefore you* (humanity)."

Upper section

Exodus 1 and ***Exodus 2***

This illustration (***BECAUSE***) depicts the biblical motive for obedience:

Left section, ***Exodus 1*** (see **ILLUSTRATION 10**; Deuteronomy 15:15). God rescued the Israelites from slavery in Egypt, and led them through the wilderness into the Promised Land.

Right section, ***Exodus 2***. The illustration contains symbols of:

a. Jesus' life (***Servant King***)
b. Jesus' crucifixion (***cross***)—in reality, His coronation (***crown above cross***)
c. Jesus' resurrection (***open and empty tomb***)
d. Jesus' ascension (***arrow rising into a cloud***)
e. The Holy Spirit (***dove***)

In the original Greek of Luke 9:31, the word translated as "departure" is *exodus*; the word translated as "accomplish" would be better translated as *complete*. Jesus' ministry was a "rescue event" which rescued humanity from the dominion of the deadly trio of Satan, sin, and death.

Lower section

This illustration (***THEREFORE***) depicts the desired human response. God wants people to ***serve one another in community***.

Since the fall into sin, human nature wants to reverse God's order of *divine action* (***BECAUSE***) and *human response* (***THEREFORE***). People view the commandments as a *merit system* rather than as a *response system* (*guidelines for saying "thank you" to God for His mercy and goodness*).

ILLUSTRATION 13

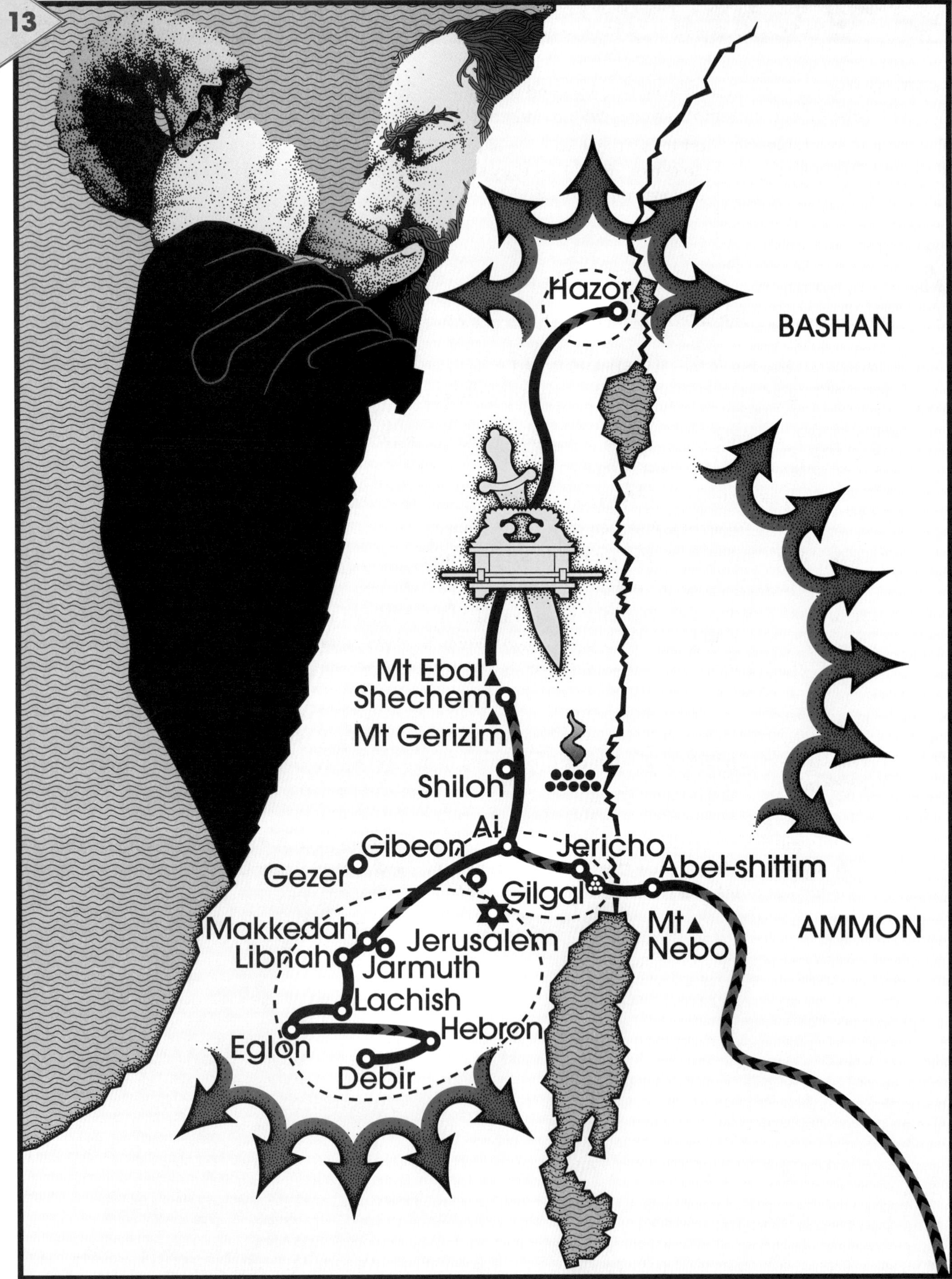

The Conquest

 Deuteronomy 34:1–8 says Moses viewed Canaan from Pisgah near ***Mt. Nebo***, and was buried in Moab near Baal-peor. Though he led the Israelites to the border of the Promised Land, he did not enter it. Joshua chs. 1–5 describe preliminaries to the conquest (depicted in **ILLUSTRATION 13**).

a. Joshua (***shown blowing a shofar or ram's horn***) is put in charge of the conquest, 1:1–9.
b. The half-tribe of Manasseh, and Gad and Reuben, who will live east of the Jordan River, are to help capture Canaan, 1:10–18. They eventually lead the invasion, ch. 3.
c. Spies are sent from ***Abel-shittim*** to Rahab the harlot at ***Jericho***, ch. 2.
d. The ***Ark of the Covenant*** opens a path through the ***Jordan River*** for the invaders, ch. 3.
e. ***Memorial stones*** are erected in the middle of the Jordan and at ***Gilgal***, ch. 4.
Later generations of Israelites did not merely recall past events; they celebrated their participation in them, Deuteronomy 6:20–25, 26:5–9; see also Romans 6:1–11.
f. All males born during the wilderness period are finally circumcised, 5:2–9.
g. A Passover is celebrated at ***Gilgal***, and the manna ceases to fall, 5:10–12.
h. God assumes leadership of the army, 5:13–15.

 Only four chapters describe the actual conquest of territory west of the Jordan. (The capture of the east bank region is described in Numbers chs. 21–36.)

a. Joshua 6 describes the capture of ***Jericho***; 7:1–5 and 8:1–29 describe the capture of ***Ai***. This region became the *territory of Benjamin* (***smaller circle west of Jordan***).
b. Joshua 10 describes the capture of what became the *territory of Judah* (***larger circle***).
c. Joshua 11 describes the capture of the *region around the northern fortress of* ***Hazor***.
d. Ch. 12 contains a list of Israel's victories, and makes references to place names not referred to elsewhere in Joshua.
e. Joshua describes the Israelites capturing the land largely by force of arms (***sword***).

 The contents of Joshua 13–24 can be summarized as follows:

a. Chs. 13–19 describe the division of the land among the tribes.
b. Cities of refuge are established—three on each side of the Jordan, ch. 20.
c. The tribe of priests known as the Levites are assigned towns in which to live, ch. 21.
d. Gad, Reuben, and the half-tribe of Manasseh return to their assigned territory east of the Jordan. A dispute erupted concerning an ***altar*** (*shown*) that they built, ch. 22.
e. Joshua makes a farewell speech, ch. 23.

Joshua leads the people in a covenant ceremony at ***Shechem***, 24:1–28; see also 8:30–35. Reference is made to Joshua's death and burial, 24:29,30. Joseph's bones are buried at Shechem, 24:32. Aaron's son, Eleazar, dies and is buried at Gibeah, 24:33.

 Though chs. 6–11 (see especially 11:23) suggest that the conquest was swift and total, other passages suggest that this was not entirely the case, 13:1,13; 15:63; 16:10; 17:12; 23:4–7,12,13.

 The account of the conquest in Joshua focuses on the following themes:

- God was the *Commander-in-chief.*
- Joshua was God's *general.*
- The conquest was carried out by a *united Israel.*
- The conquest was *swift.*
- The conquest was *complete.*

ILLUSTRATION
14

Gods—Ancient and Modern

After the Israelites conquered and settled in the land, the book of Judges (to be studied next) reports that many of them worshiped false gods, referred to as the Baals and Ashtaroth (***male and female idols***, **ILLUSTRATION 14**).

 Why did they do this?

a. Though the nations around Israel worshiped similar gods (both male and female), each nation gave them different names: Baal and Astarte, Ishtar and Tammuz, Isis and Osiris. In **ILLUSTRATION 14**, these gods are depicted by the ***large male and female figures*** (*top center*).

b. Ancient peoples made molten or carved ***images*** of these gods, and sometimes made them out of clay or terracotta (***idols***, *top left and right*). The images had highly accentuated sexual features. The gods they represented were personifications of the forces of nature.

c. Fertility religions did not focus on covenants and commandments (***hence, symbols for these are canceled out***, *bottom right*). Their concern was to make sure that crops yielded well to provide for humanity's physical needs (***approval sign over grain crops***, *bottom center*).

d. Adherents to these ancient religions believed that when rain fell to the ground, the ***male god*** (*top left*) who lived in the ***clouds and sky*** (*center*) was inseminating the ***female goddess*** (*top right*) who lived in and symbolized the earth.

e. Those who practiced these religions (***small male and female figures***, *bottom left*) also believed they could manipulate the gods into having sexual relations if men had sexual relations with a sacred prostitute in a shrine or temple. The human action was intended to persuade the male and female gods (***large male and female figures***, *top center*) to have sex so that the rains would fall and the crops would grow.

 It is important to remember that when the Israelites lived in Egypt, they had access to a reliable water supply from the Nile River and used irrigation to water their crops, vines, and orchards. However, when the Israelites entered Canaan, they had to learn new farming methods—and naturally asked the Canaanites how they might obtain water for their crops. The answers the Canaanites gave them prompted the Israelites to embrace the Canaanite religious beliefs and practices—for their very survival was at stake. No rain, no crops. No crops, no food. No food, no life!

A central thought that weaves its way through the biblical materials is this: We cannot *manipulate* the God revealed in the Bible in relation to fertility and salvation. We can only *submit* to that God.

ILLUSTRATION 15

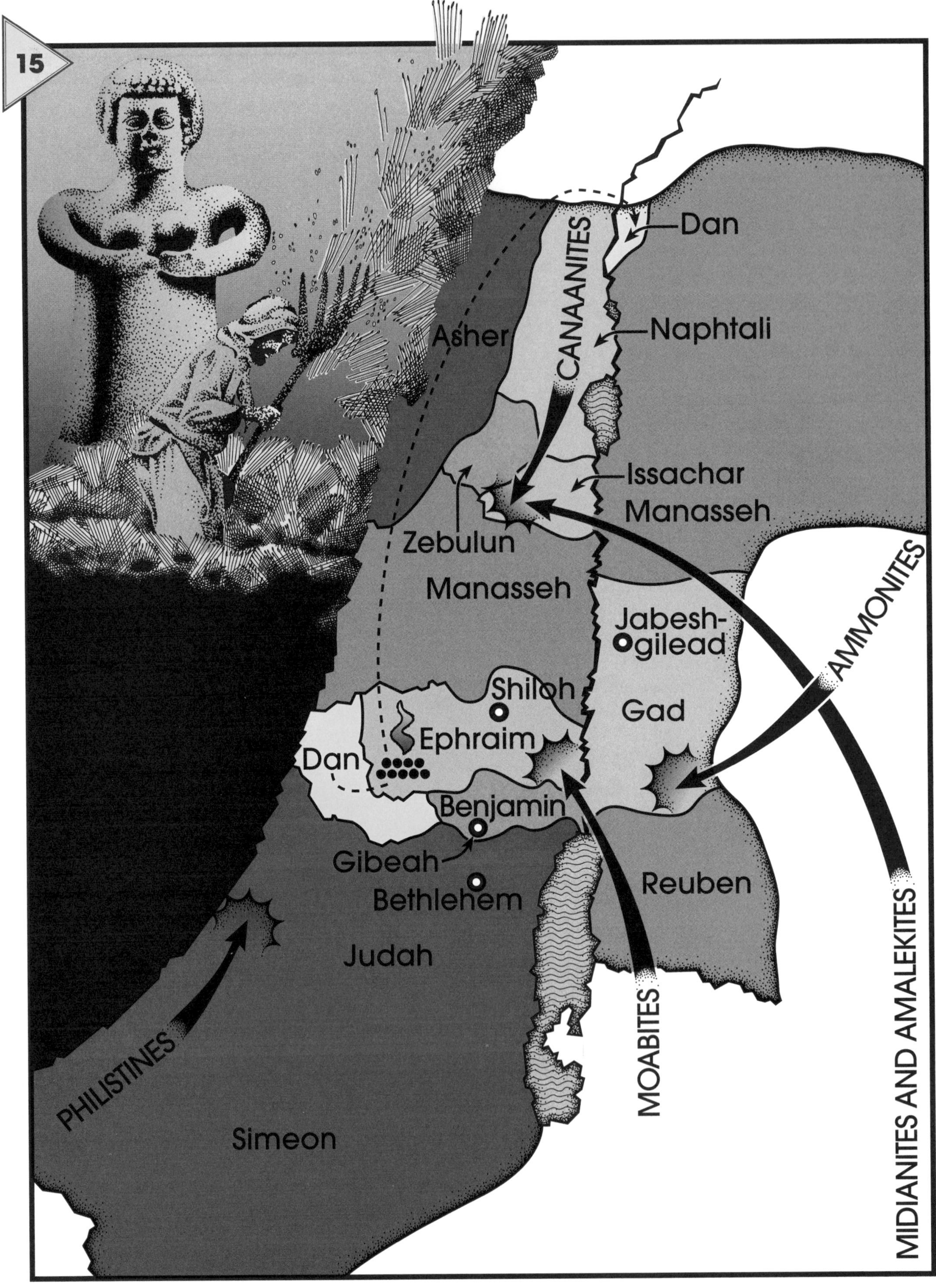

A Fragmented Israel

Some scholars suggest that the description of the conquest in Joshua is rather idealized. They believe it focuses on how the Israelites *should have undertaken the conquest rather than on how they did*. They further suggest that Judges 1:1–2:10 describes *what actually happened*, with each tribe *individually* attempting to capture the territory assigned to it. (Note that Joshua's death is reported twice, Joshua 24:29,30; Judges 2:6–10.)

After settling in the land, the Israelites had to face harassment from surviving Canaanites and from nations living on its borders. Judges says these attacks took place because ***the Israelites were forsaking the Lord and worshiping the Baals*** (**ILLUSTRATION 15**, *top left*). The challenge that the prophet Elijah eventually issued to the priests and worshipers of the Baals on Mt. Carmel was the end result of a long, previous history, 1 Kings 18; note v. 21.

A continuing cycle (***A-B-C-D***) runs through Judges chs. 1–16:

- ***Apostasy:*** The people sin.
- ***Battered:*** The Lord disciplines His people.
- ***Cry:*** The people cry to the Lord for help.
- ***Deliverance:*** The Lord raises up a judge to rescue His people from their oppressors.

Judges makes reference to thirteen judges from nine different tribes leading the people into battle against their enemies. The *major* narratives (see ***arrows*** on **ILLUSTRATION 15**) describe how:

- Ehud rescued Israel from the ***Moabites***, 3:12–30.
- Deborah and Barak rescued Israel from the ***Canaanites***, chs. 4,5.
- Gideon rescued Israel from the ***Midianites and Amalekites***, chs. 6–8.
- Jephthah rescued Israel from the ***Ammonites***, chs. 10–12.
- Samson fought the ***Philistines***, chs. 13–16.

Judges chs. 17,18 relate how ***a place of worship (altar with flame at top) in Ephraim was transferred to Dan***, at the northern tip of the Israelites' realm; the writer(s) of 1 and 2 Kings show a negative attitude toward this shrine; see 1 Kings 12:25–33 and 13:33,34.

Judges chs. 19–21 describe a horrible crime. When a Levite and his concubine were returning from Bethlehem to Ephraim, men in ***Gibeah*** of ***Benjamin*** (later, Saul's capital) raped and killed the concubine. In the ensuing battle, the men of other Israelite tribes killed all but 600 of the men of Benjamin. Wives were then found for these survivors in ***Jabesh-gilead*** and ***Shiloh***. (It is significant that later, King Saul, a Benjaminite, was quick to go to the rescue of Jabesh-gilead, 1 Samuel 11; perhaps one of Saul's ancestors came from there. Furthermore, eventually the men of Jabesh-gilead provided a decent burial for the bodies of Saul and his sons, 1 Samuel 31.)

Judges hints that the Israelites must do three things:

- Create *unity* among the tribes.
- Establish *continuity* of rule—by kings, perhaps?
- Maintain *purity* of faith—worship the God of the exodus, not the Baals.

The lack of leadership created problems among the people: "In those days *there was no king in Israel*; all the people did what was right in their own eyes," 17:6; see also 18:1, 19:1, 21:25.

ILLUSTRATION 16

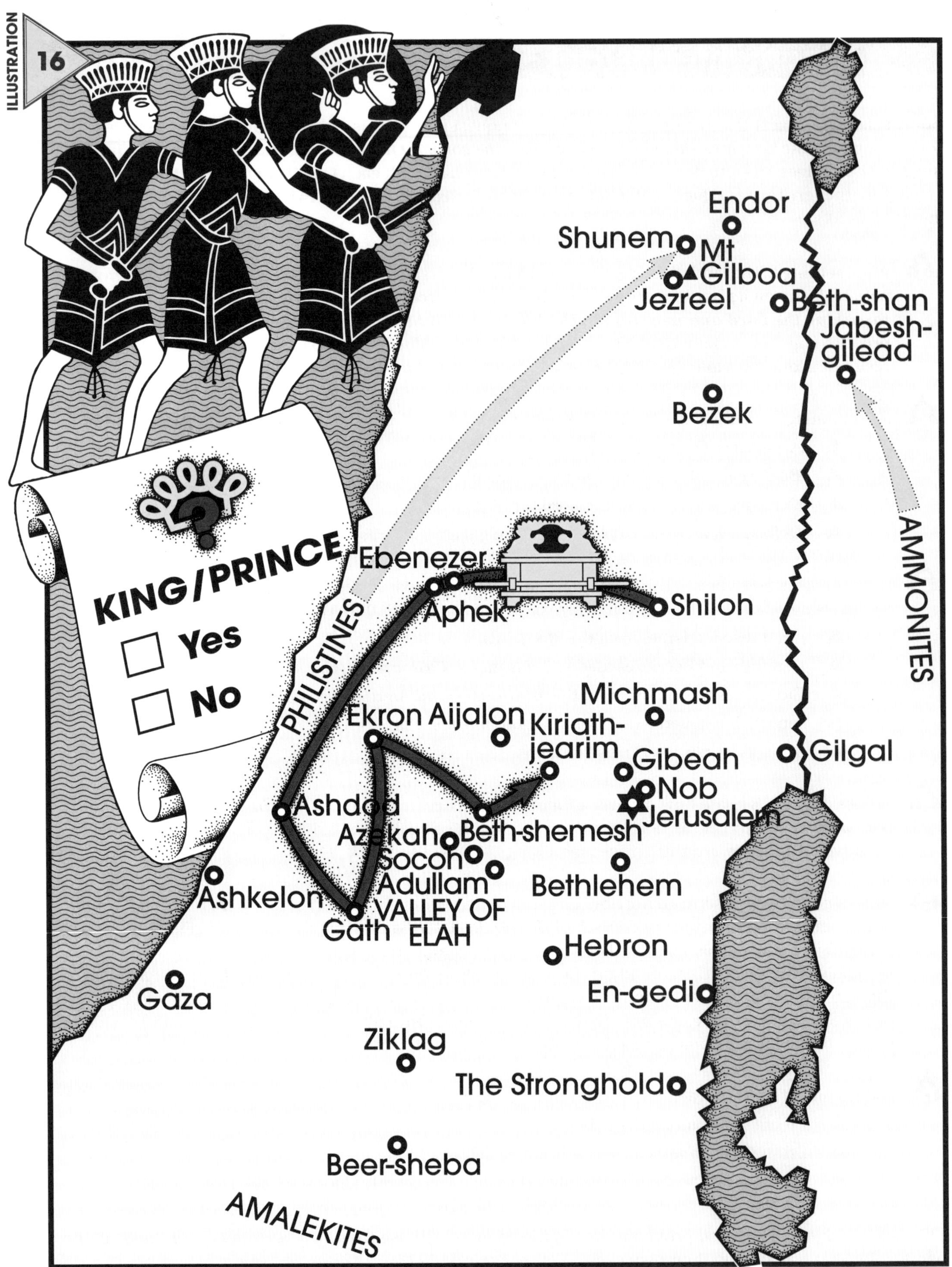

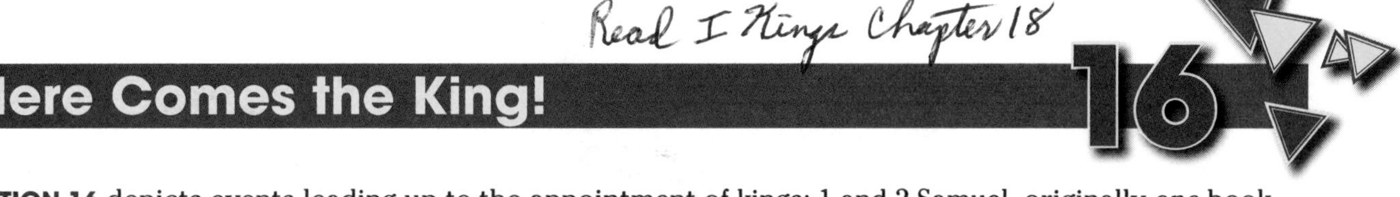

Here Comes the King!

ILLUSTRATION 16 depicts events leading up to the appointment of kings; 1 and 2 Samuel, originally *one* book, were divided into *two* books when the Old Testament was translated into Greek about 250 B.C. These books cover Israel's history from the birth of Samuel to the time when David's life was drawing to an end (about 1070–960 B.C.). All references below are from 1 Samuel unless otherwise indicated.

Chs. 1–6: The opening scene takes place at ***Shiloh*** where the ***Ark of the Covenant*** was kept. The priest there was Eli, who was assisted by his two sons (who were corrupt, 2:12–17, 22–25) and eventually Samuel. After the ***Philistines*** (*top left*) captured the Ark in the battle of ***Aphek***, the Ark was taken to several Philistine cities (***Ashdod***, ***Gath***, ***Ekron***; possibly also ***Ashkelon*** and ***Gaza***) and caused their inhabitants great physical discomfort. The Philistines eventually sent the Ark back to Israel where, after a brief stay at ***Beth-shemesh*** (6:12,19,20), it was welcomed and cared for in ***Kiriath-jearim***, 6:21–7:2.

After telling us that Samuel's sons were also corrupt (8:1–3), and speaking negatively about the role of kings in general (ch. 8), chs. 9–11 describe the appointment of *Saul of Benjamin* as king.

a. Initially, Samuel anointed Saul *privately*, and then ate with him, 9:1–10:16. Remarkably, the spirit of God came upon Saul, 10:9–13; 19:23,24 (but note also 1 Samuel 16:14).

b. Later, Samuel anointed Saul *publicly*, 10:17–27.

c. After some expressed doubts about Saul's ability to lead the people (10:27), Saul responded by gathering an army at ***Bezek*** and rescuing the people of ***Jabesh-gilead*** from the ***Ammonites***, 10:27b–11:11. After demonstrating his leadership qualities in this manner, Saul was again declared king at ***Gilgal***, 11:12–15.

To understand the "***yes*** or ***no***" debate in chs. 8–11 about whether or not to have kings (***crown***, ***question mark***), it is helpful to note that some passages refer to the coming ruler as "**prince**" or "leader" (*always* favorably), others as "**king**" (*sometimes* unfavorably, for *God alone is King!*).

Saul fell from Samuel's favor for two reasons: he grew impatient when Samuel did not arrive in time to offer sacrifice prior to battle (1 Samuel 10:8; 13:1–15), and on another occasion spared the life of Agag the ***Amalekite*** in a "holy war," 1 Samuel 15. Samuel then secretly anointed *David of Judah* to replace Saul as king of Israel. From that point on, all debate about the advisability of having a king ceased. The issue was merely how long it would be before David (from *Judah*), a "man after God's own heart," 13:14, took over from Saul (from *Benjamin*).

David joined Saul's staff as his armor-bearer and musician, ch. 16. First Samuel 17:1,2 describes the Philistines and Israelites gathering at ***Socoh***, ***Azekah***, and the ***Valley of Elah*** for battle—a battle in which David killed Goliath (ch. 17; but note 2 Samuel 21:19). Beyond this point, the narrative in 1 Samuel traces the demise of Saul and the rise of David.

Saul had to deal with frequent Philistine attacks on his territory. His final battle with them is described in chs. 28–31. After Saul consulted a witch at ***Endor*** (and ate with her, 28:20–25!), his forces fought the Philistines in the vicinity of ***Mt. Gilboa***. Three of Saul's sons were killed in the battle (but see also 1 Chronicles 10:6), and Saul committed suicide.

The Philistines beheaded Saul, and suspended his body from the walls surrounding ***Beth-shan***. The people of ***Jabesh-gilead*** (to whom Saul had shown mercy early in his reign, ch. 11) showed mercy to Saul by providing decent burial for his body and those of his sons.

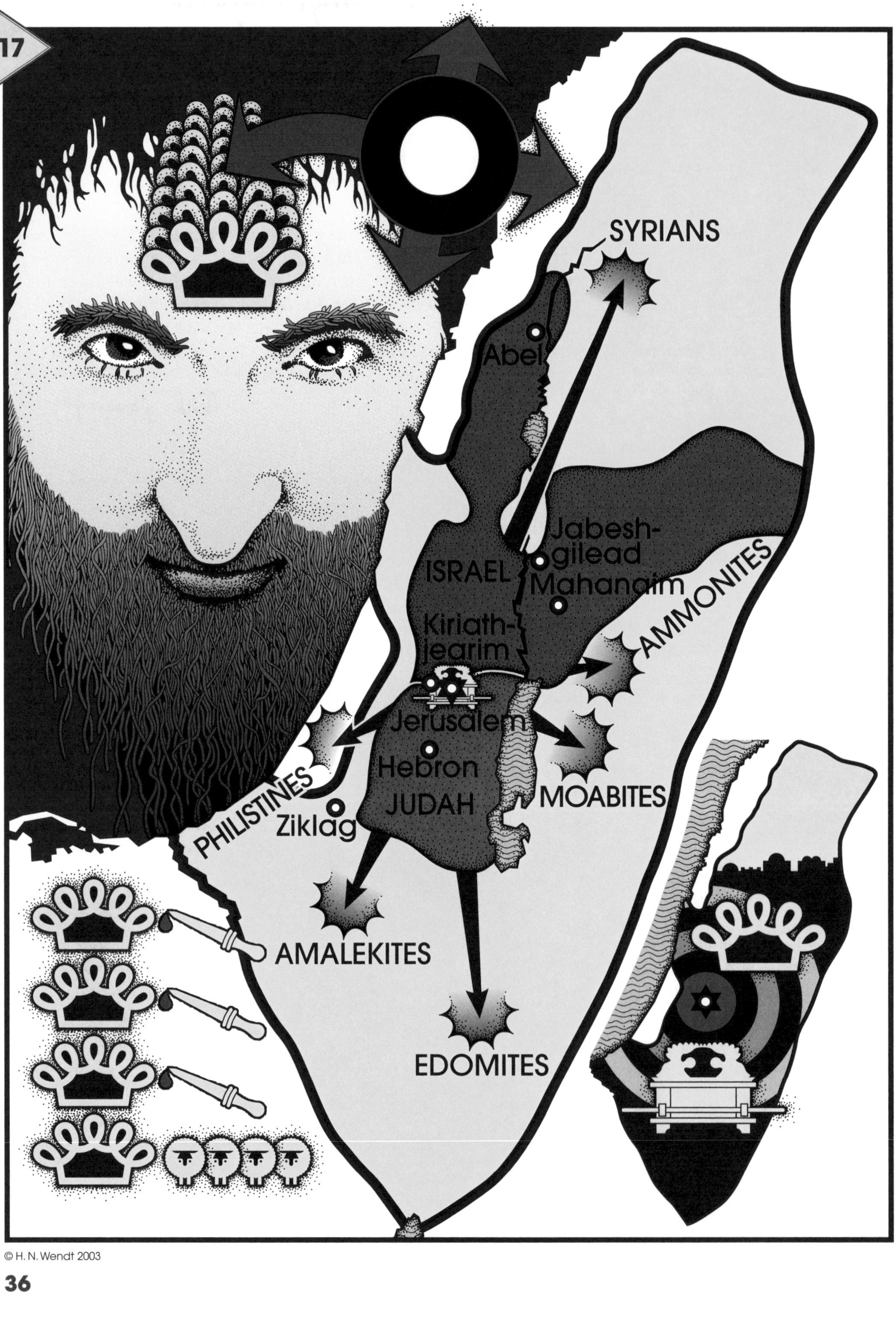

17

SYRIANS
Abel
Jabesh-gilead
ISRAEL
Mahanaim
AMMONITES
Kiriath-jearim
Jerusalem
Hebron
PHILISTINES
JUDAH
MOABITES
Ziklag
AMALEKITES
EDOMITES

David

 After Saul's death (1 Samuel 31), ***David*** (***face***, *top left*, **ILLUSTRATION 17**) was made king of Judah at ***Hebron*** (2 Samuel 2:1–4). However, the leaders of Israel met at ***Jabesh-gilead*** and decided they did not want to submit to David as their king, 2 Samuel 2:4b–11. It took David another seven years to gain control over the northern area, 2 Samuel 3:1–5:5.

 After gaining control of both Judah and Israel, David decided he needed a new capital. He therefore took ***Jerusalem*** from the Jebusites (2 Samuel 5:6–10), made it his capital and called it "the city of David," v. 9. During the campaign, David gave orders that its defenders ("the blind and the lame") were to be put to death, v. 8a. From that day on, no blind or lame person was permitted to enter the Temple, v. 8b. (But note Luke 2:4 and Matthew 21:14.) David then built himself a palace in the city, (2 Samuel 5: 11,12), and brought the ***Ark of the Covenant*** from ***Kiriath-jearim*** to Jerusalem, 2 Samuel 6. The Ark was housed in a specially built tent, 6:17.

 The Lord said "No!" to David's suggestion that he should build God a Temple, and stated that He, the Lord, would build a "house" (*a dynasty or line of kings*, ***row of crowns***) out of David that would last "forever," 2 Samuel 7; note the word "forever" in 7:13,16,25,29.

 It is customary to praise David's so-called saintly qualities. However, numerous passages suggest that David was something of a political animal, 1 Samuel 27:8–12; 30:26 (bribery); 2 Samuel 3:2–5; 5:13–16; 6: 20–23; chs. 11,12; ch. 20; ch. 21; 1 Kings 2:1–9.

 David's family was seriously dysfunctional. After David's adultery with Bathsheba and murder of Uriah (chs. 11,12), Nathan told him a story about a rich man who owned many sheep, but stole the one lamb a poor man owned. David insisted that the rich man give the poor man ***four lambs*** (*bottom left*), 12: 1–6; see Exodus 22:1. Ironically, David himself lost "four lambs": his first son by Bathsheba, 12:15–19; Amnon, ch. 13; Absalom, 18:1–18, and Adonijah, 1 Kings 2:13–25.

 David built his empire in a brutal manner. For example, the Benjaminite, Sheba, who revolted against David was beheaded at ***Abel***, 2 Samuel 20. David permitted the Gibeonites to impale two of his brothers-in-law and five of his nephews, 2 Samuel 21. On his death bed, he asked Solomon to kill Joab (his nephew and former general) and Shimei—who had cursed him when he fled from Absalom, 2 Samuel 16:5–14 (despite the fact that he had assured a repentant Shimei that he would not harm him, 2 Samuel 19:16–23); see 1 Kings 2:1–9.

 2 Samuel 13–1 Kings 2:46 describes the struggle for the throne among David's sons (***four crowns***, ***three daggers***, *bottom left*.) Absalom killed *Amnon*, 2 Sam. 13. When *Absalom* revolted, his cousin Joab killed him 2 Sam. 15–18. After Nathan and Bathsheba persuaded David to declare *Solomon* his successor, Solomon killed his older brother, *Adonijah*, 1 Kings 1:11–40, 2:13–25.

 2 Samuel 5:17–25 reports how David subdued the ***Philistines***, and chs. 8 and 10 describe how he expanded the nation's borders by conquering the neighboring ***Syrians***, ***Ammonites***, ***Moabites***, ***Edomites***, and ***Amalekites***.

 1 Samuel 13:14 and 1 and 2 Kings (e.g. 1 Kings 11:4,6 and 2 Kings 22:2), characterize David as "a man after God's own heart"—that is, *he captured Jerusalem and established it as the nation's capital and most important worship center.* The key thought is: **David worshiped one God—and he worshiped that God in Jerusalem.** The illustration at *bottom right* depicts ***David's realm,*** a ***crown***, a ***bull's eye*** highlighting the *location of Jerusalem* (***star***), ***Jerusalem's skyline***, and the ***Ark of the Covenant***. David's dynasty lasted from about 1,000 to 587 B.C.

ILLUSTRATION 18

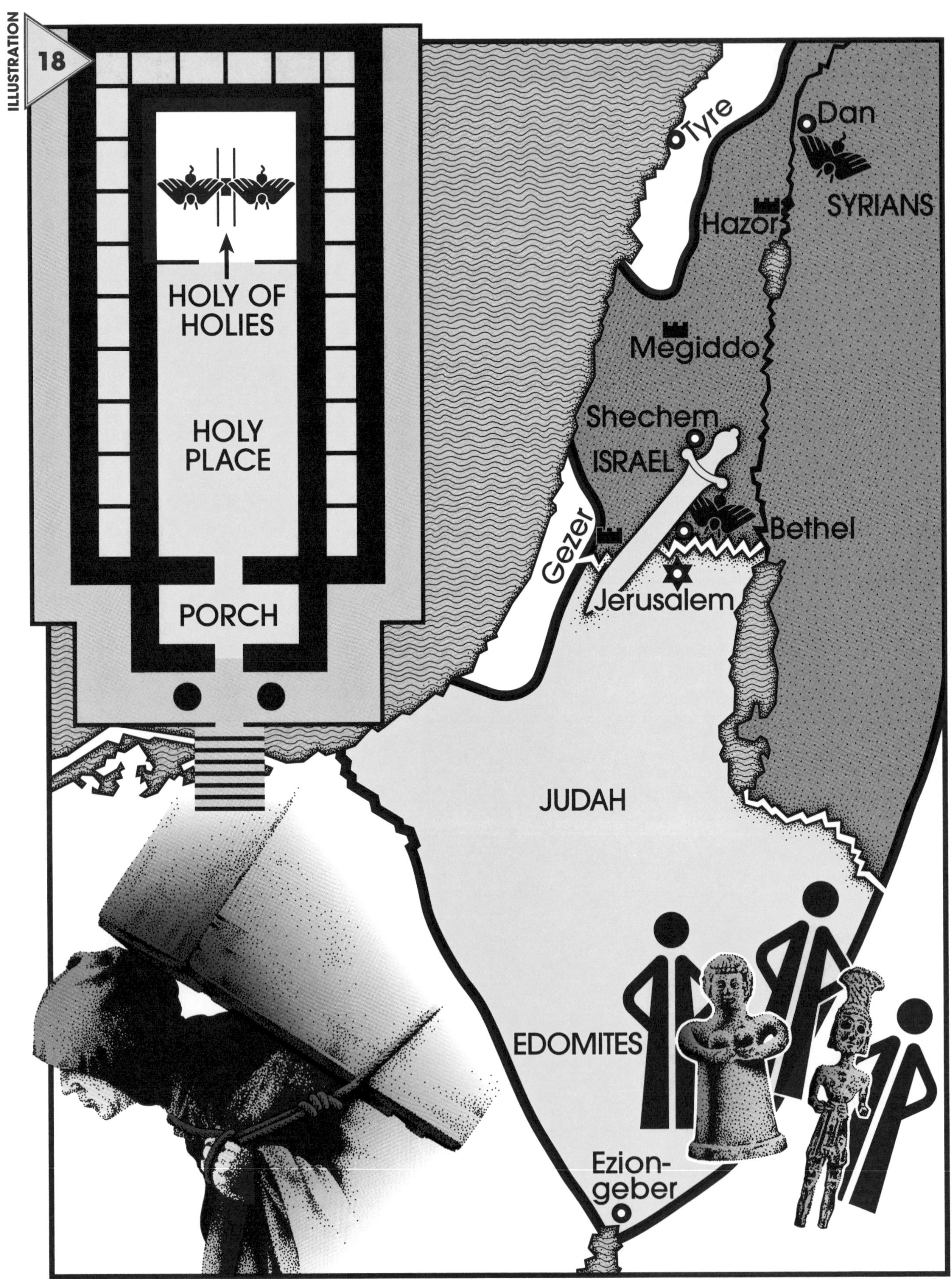

Solomon

Prior to David's death, Bathsheba persuaded David to appoint her son Solomon as his successor, 1 Kings 1:15–31. After being made king, Solomon killed his brother Adonijah, his cousin Joab (David's general), and Shimei—who had once cursed David (2 Samuel 16:5–14; but note 2 Samuel 19:16–23); see 1 Kings 2:19–46. He sent Abiathar, a priest, into exile in Anathoth, 2:26,27. Both Joab and Abiathar had endorsed Adonijah as David's successor, 1:7.

The writer of 1 Kings showed great interest in Solomon's wisdom (4:29–34, 10:23,24), international trading ventures (9:26–28), and foreign visitors, 10:1–13. (All texts are from 1 Kings unless indicated.)

ILLUSTRATION 18 summarizes events during Solomon's reign. His building ventures, most of them in Jerusalem (chs. 6,7), took twenty years to complete, 6:38; 7:1; see also 9:15–22; 10:14–22. Solomon built a ***Temple*** in ***Jerusalem***, and placed the ***Ark of the Covenant*** and ***two cherubim*** in its innermost sanctuary, the ***Holy of Holies***. He also built two palaces—one for himself and one for the Egyptian wife who was apparently his most important spouse, 7:8. Hiram of ***Tyre*** provided him with building materials and workers for these projects. Solomon paid Hiram for his services by giving him a northern segment of the Promised Land, 9:10–14.

Solomon built ***fortresses*** at ***Hazor***, ***Megiddo***, and ***Gezer***, 9:15. ***Hazor*** was located on an important highway leading from Syria to Egypt, ***Megiddo*** on the plain of Jezreel where many battles were fought over the centuries, and ***Gezer*** on the road leading from the Mediterranean coast to Jerusalem. Solomon also made money by selling weapons, 10:26–29.

Solomon established ***Ezion-geber*** as a port city, and worked together with the Phoenicians to make it a strategic location for trading ventures to eastern countries, 9:26–29. (There was, after all, no Suez Canal at that point in history!)

Internally, Solomon's building programs were achieved at a price—the sweat and blood of his people (***person carrying burden***, *bottom left*); see 4:6; 5:13–18; 9:15; 12:4,14.

He did away with what was left of the old tribal boundaries, and divided the realm into districts to serve the needs of his Jerusalem-based administrative system, 4:7–19,22–28.

To cap it all off, Solomon dabbled in idolatry, 11:1–8. He erected shrines to, and worshiped, the gods of his many foreign wives (***female figures and idols***, *bottom right*).

Though some rated Solomon's achievements highly (4:25), others were not so enthusiastic, Deuteronomy 17:14–17; 1 Samuel 8:10–18. Already during Solomon's lifetime, the ***Syrians*** and ***Edomites*** rebelled against Israel and gained political independence, 11:14–25.

Solomon's son, Rehoboam, succeeded his father as king of ***Judah*** (***yellow section***) and then went to ***Shechem*** to try to gain control of the northern region—later to be called ***Israel***. However, when he refused to lighten the burdens of the northerners, they revolted, separated from Judah (***sword***, ***fragmenting lines***), and established their own line of kings, the first of whom was Jeroboam, 12:1–24. **A united kingdom was torn apart (*sword*) to become a divided kingdom—JUDAH** (Southern Kingdom, ***yellow section***) **and ISRAEL** (Northern Kingdom, ***orange section***).

Early in his reign, Jeroboam established shrines at ***Dan*** and ***Bethel***, 12:25–33; see 2 Kings 10:28–31. The writers of Kings hated these shrines, for they diverted the northerners from worshiping at the Temple in Jerusalem. Though they attacked them as "idolatrous," the real issue was that **those who worshiped at Dan and Bethel no longer worshiped in Jerusalem!**

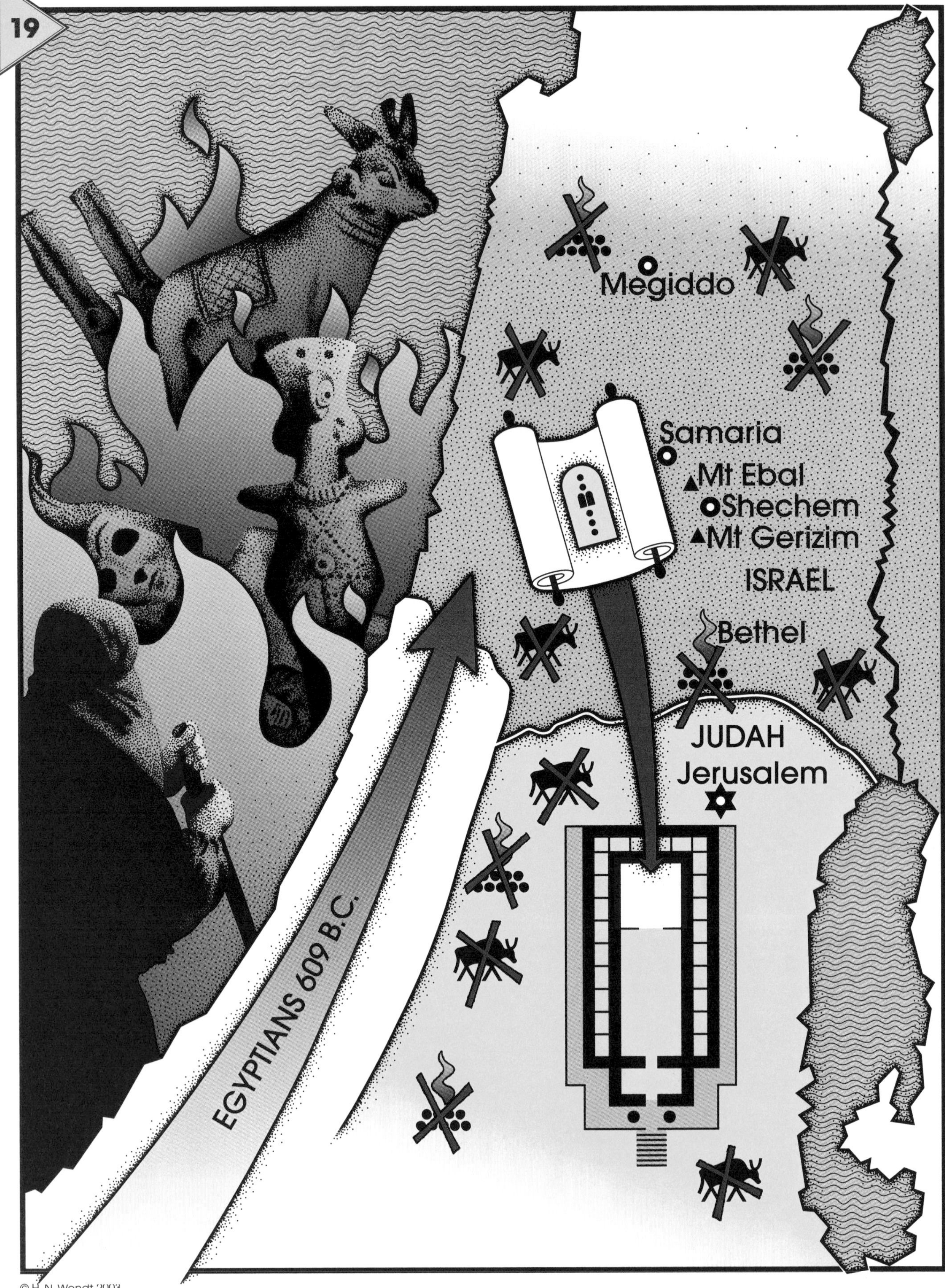
Megiddo
Samaria
Mt Ebal
Shechem
Mt Gerizim
ISRAEL
Bethel
JUDAH
Jerusalem
EGYPTIANS 609 B.C.

Josiah: One God—One Place

ILLUSTRATION 19 depicts the events outlined in 2 Kings chs. 22,23: The centralization of worship and the sacrificial system in the Jerusalem Temple in 621 B.C. (All texts are from 2 Kings, unless indicated.)

In 621 B.C., Josiah, King of Judah, arranged to have the ***Temple*** repaired, 22:3. While these repairs were in progress, the high priest Hilkiah found "the book of the law" (***scroll, with symbol for covenant superimposed***) in the Temple; the book was read to the king, 22:8–10. Josiah had Huldah the prophetess provide him with an interpretation of the book's message, 22:14–20. The heart of that message was, "God's people must worship one God in one place." Josiah then led a covenant ceremony in which he pledged "to follow the Lord, keeping his commandments, his decrees, and his statutes, with all his heart and all his soul, to perform the words of this covenant that were written in this book." All present joined in the ritual, 23:1–3. The events which followed were of great importance.

Josiah removed from the Temple objects used in Baal worship and Assyrian astral worship, burned them (***calf***, ***idol***, ***image***, ***royal worker***, *left*), and dumped their ashes at ***Bethel***—formerly the royal shrine of the Northern Kingdom, Amos 7:10–12, 2 Kings 23:4,5. Southern priests hated Bethel. They insisted that God's people should worship the one God in one place—***Jerusalem***!

Josiah closed all shrines in Judah, leaving the Jerusalem Temple as the only legitimate place for offering sacrifice. Some of the outlying shrines were most likely shrines in which the God of Israel was worshiped—even though their priests were referred to as "idolatrous," 23:5. After all, any "orthodox" shrine located outside of Jerusalem was now viewed as "idolatrous." Other shrines were certainly pagan; the people worshiped the Baals and Assyrian astral deities in them, 23:5b. (In **ILLUSTRATION 19**, *orthodox shrines* are depicted by an ***altar of stones***; *pagan shrines* are depicted by a ***bull***. All are ***crossed out***—to signify that they are all now considered invalid.)

Josiah then cleansed Jerusalem—and the Temple—of Baal worship, male temple prostitutes, women who wove hangings for the fertility goddesses, child sacrifice, horses and chariots dedicated to the sun, altars linked to Ahaz and Manasseh, the idolatrous shrines that Solomon had built some 300 years earlier, and mediums, wizards, teraphim, idols, and other abominations, 23:6–14,24.

Next, King Josiah smashed *all shrines in what had been the Northern Kingdom*, killed all the priests who served at them (they were not Levites, 1 Kings 12:31), and burned human bones on the altars to defile them, 23:15–20. It is likely that the God of Israel was worshiped at many of these shrines, for the issue had to do with **centralization, geographical validity, control, and the growing power of the Jerusalem priests.**

Finally, Josiah commanded that a Passover celebration be held in Jerusalem—now the only valid shrine, 23:21–23. Most likely, the book of the law that gave rise to Josiah's reform had previously been used in the Northern Kingdom (before its destruction by the Assyrians in 721 B.C.) in an attempt to centralize worship in Israel at ***Shechem*** or on ***Mt. Gerizim*** (which eventually became the "Holy Mountain" for the Samaritans). See Deut.12:2–7,11,14,18,21,26; 14,23–25; 16:2,6,7,11,15.

Josiah was killed in ***609 B.C.*** at ***Megiddo*** while trying to prevent the ***Egyptians from marching north*** to prop up a crumbling Assyria as a buffer against an expanding Babylonian empire, 23:28–30.

The fact that all sacrifices now had to be offered in the Jerusalem Temple gave rise to a system of animal sellers and money changers. In Jesus' day, 9,000 priests and Levites served on the Temple's staff. Anyone who attacked its "sin management system," its "salvation marketing system," was asking for trouble. **Jesus' attack cost Him His life!**

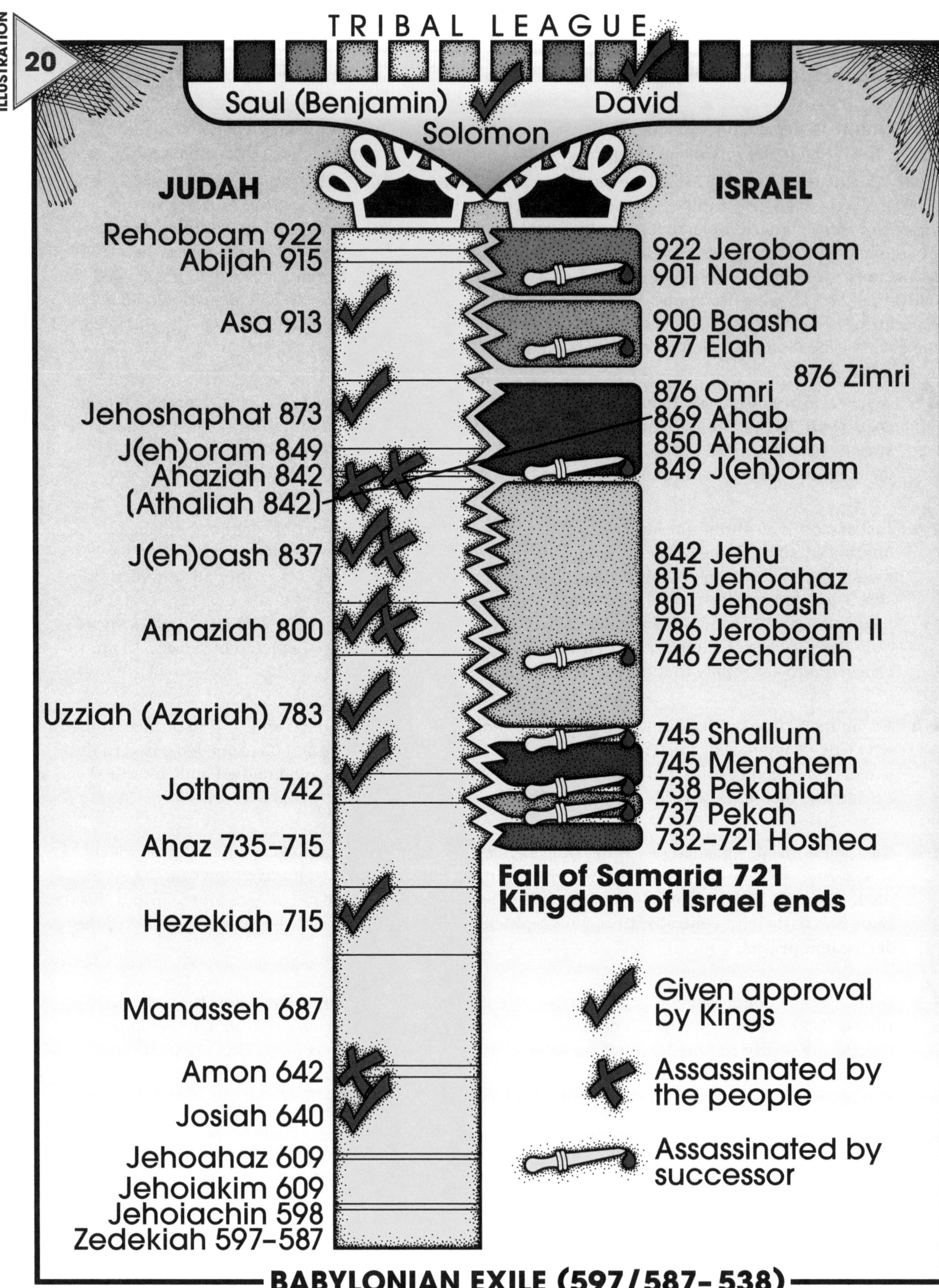
ILLUSTRATION
20
TRIBAL LEAGUE
Saul (Benjamin)
David
Solomon
JUDAH
ISRAEL
Rehoboam 922
Abijah 915
Asa 913
Jehoshaphat 873
J(eh)oram 849
Ahaziah 842
(Athaliah 842)
J(eh)oash 837
Amaziah 800
Uzziah (Azariah) 783
Jotham 742
Ahaz 735–715
Hezekiah 715
Manasseh 687
Amon 642
Josiah 640
Jehoahaz 609
Jehoiakim 609
Jehoiachin 598
Zedekiah 597–587
922 Jeroboam
901 Nadab
900 Baasha
877 Elah
876 Zimri
876 Omri
869 Ahab
850 Ahaziah
849 J(eh)oram
842 Jehu
815 Jehoahaz
801 Jehoash
786 Jeroboam II
746 Zechariah
745 Shallum
745 Menahem
738 Pekahiah
737 Pekah
732–721 Hoshea
Fall of Samaria 721
Kingdom of Israel ends
Given approval by Kings
Assassinated by the people
Assassinated by successor
BABYLONIAN EXILE (597/587–538)

Dynasties and Kingdoms

ILLUSTRATION 20 lists the kings who ruled:

- The United Kingdom: 3 kings (***Saul***, ***David***, ***Solomon***).
- The Northern Kingdom, ***ISRAEL***: 19 kings.
- The Southern Kingdom, ***JUDAH***: 19 kings, plus upstart Queen ***Athaliah***, daughter of the northern king, ***Ahab***, and his Phoenician wife, Jezebel. Athaliah ruled Judah for about six years, 2 Kings 11:1–21; see v.1–3. Note ***the line linking Athaliah to Ahab***.

The United Kingdom

a. How long ***Saul*** reigned is uncertain, 1 Samuel 13:1. His son, Ishbosheth, ruled for several years, 2 Samuel 2:10,11.

b. ***David*** ruled Judah for about seven years, and the United Kingdom for about 33 years.

c. ***Solomon*** ruled the United Kingdom for about 40 years.

The Divided Kingdom—ISRAEL

a. Nine dynasties (denoted by ***colored blocks***) ruled Israel; four consisted of only one ruler.

b. In seven cases, dynastic change was brought about by assassination (***daggers***). ***Zimri*** committed suicide after ruling for only seven days (1 Kings 16:8–20) and ***Shallum*** reigned for only one month, 2 Kings 15:8–15; neither has a colored block in **ILLUSTRATION 20**.

c. ***The Assyrians destroyed Israel in 721 B.C.***

The Divided Kingdom—JUDAH

a. One dynasty, David's, ruled in Judah (exception: ***Athaliah***; see 2 Kings 11).

b. The continuing Davidic dynasty contributed toward political stability in Judah, and enabled the southern realm to survive longer than its northern neighbor.

c. The writer of 1 and 2 Kings commends or condemns each king on the basis of the attitude he adopted toward Jerusalem and its Temple. He disapproves of all northern kings because they encouraged worship at shrines other than the Jerusalem Temple, 1 Kings 12:25–33. He approves of some southern kings only because they repaired the Jerusalem Temple or reformed the worship life practiced within it, 1 Kings 3:1–3; 11:4–8; 2 Kings 18:1–8 (Hezekiah); 22:2, 23:25 (Josiah).

d. Although five kings of Judah were assassinated, no change in dynasty took place. ***Ahaziah*** of Judah was killed by ***Jehu*** of Israel. The other four assassinations were carried out by people within Judah—who then placed a legitimate descendant of David on the throne.

e. The ***Babylonians took exiles from Judah to Babylon in 597 B.C.*** (including 18 year-old King ***Jehoiachin***) and again in ***587 B.C.*** (including King ***Zedekiah*** whom they blinded, and whose sons they killed), 2 Kings 24:10–12; ch. 25.

According to 2 Kings 25:27–30, Jehoiachin was still alive in Babylon in 560 B.C. Without doubt, the hope developed that he would live through the exile, return to Judah and Jerusalem, and reestablish the Davidic dynasty. However, he did not return, but died in Babylon. To understand this is to begin to understand the significance of Matthew 1:1 (especially in the NRSV translation) which states that Jesus was a descendant of David! In Jesus the Messiah, the Davidic dynasty was being restored—but in a form very different from what the people were expecting! **Jesus, David's Final Descendant, washed feet, and calls His followers to do the same,** John 13:1–17, 31–35.

ILLUSTRATION 21

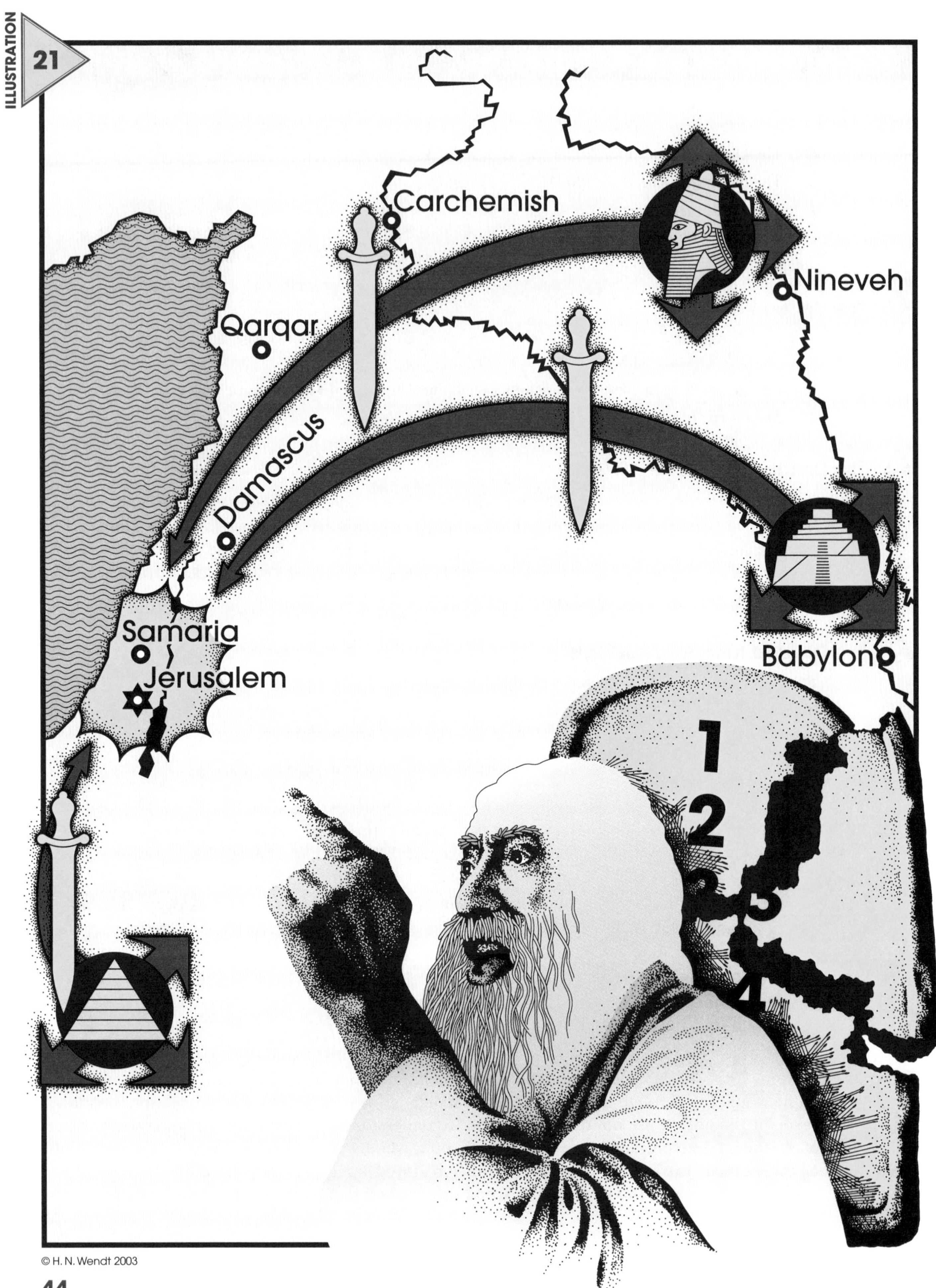

ILLUSTRATION 21

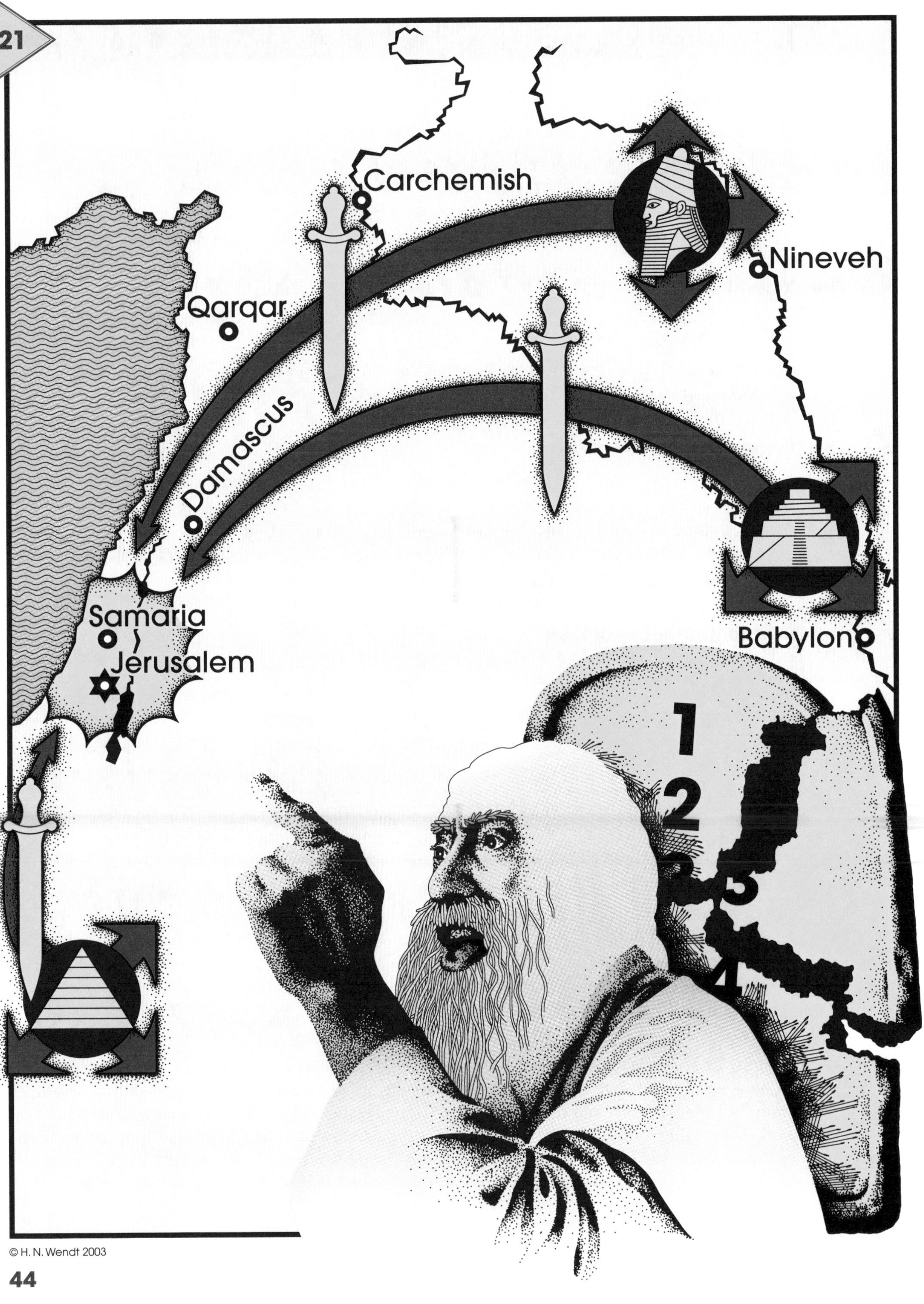

Carchemish
Nineveh
Qarqar
Damascus
Samaria
Jerusalem
Babylon
1
2
3
4
5

Dynasties and Kingdoms

ILLUSTRATION 20 lists the kings who ruled:

- The United Kingdom: 3 kings (***Saul***, ***David***, ***Solomon***).
- The Northern Kingdom, ***ISRAEL***: 19 kings.
- The Southern Kingdom, ***JUDAH***: 19 kings, plus upstart Queen ***Athaliah***, daughter of the northern king, ***Ahab***, and his Phoenician wife, Jezebel. Athaliah ruled Judah for about six years, 2 Kings 11:1–21; see v.1–3. Note ***the line linking Athaliah to Ahab***.

 The United Kingdom

a. How long ***Saul*** reigned is uncertain, 1 Samuel 13:1. His son, Ishbosheth, ruled for several years, 2 Samuel 2:10,11.

b. ***David*** ruled Judah for about seven years, and the United Kingdom for about 33 years.

c. ***Solomon*** ruled the United Kingdom for about 40 years.

 The Divided Kingdom—ISRAEL

a. Nine dynasties (denoted by ***colored blocks***) ruled Israel; four consisted of only one ruler.

b. In seven cases, dynastic change was brought about by assassination (***daggers***). ***Zimri*** committed suicide after ruling for only seven days (1 Kings 16:8–20) and ***Shallum*** reigned for only one month, 2 Kings 15:8–15; neither has a colored block in **ILLUSTRATION 20**.

c. ***The Assyrians destroyed Israel in 721 B.C.***

 The Divided Kingdom—JUDAH

a. One dynasty, David's, ruled in Judah (exception: ***Athaliah***; see 2 Kings 11).

b. The continuing Davidic dynasty contributed toward political stability in Judah, and enabled the southern realm to survive longer than its northern neighbor.

c. The writer of 1 and 2 Kings commends or condemns each king on the basis of the attitude he adopted toward Jerusalem and its Temple. He disapproves of all northern kings because they encouraged worship at shrines other than the Jerusalem Temple, 1 Kings 12:25–33. He approves of some southern kings only because they repaired the Jerusalem Temple or reformed the worship life practiced within it, 1 Kings 3:1–3; 11:4–8; 2 Kings 18:1–8 (Hezekiah); 22:2, 23:25 (Josiah).

d. Although five kings of Judah were assassinated, no change in dynasty took place. ***Ahaziah*** of Judah was killed by ***Jehu*** of Israel. The other four assassinations were carried out by people within Judah—who then placed a legitimate descendant of David on the throne.

e. The ***Babylonians took exiles from Judah to Babylon in 597 B.C.*** (including 18 year-old King ***Jehoiachin***) and again in ***587 B.C.*** (including King ***Zedekiah*** whom they blinded, and whose sons they killed), 2 Kings 24:10–12; ch. 25.

According to 2 Kings 25:27–30, Jehoiachin was still alive in Babylon in 560 B.C. Without doubt, the hope developed that he would live through the exile, return to Judah and Jerusalem, and reestablish the Davidic dynasty. However, he did not return, but died in Babylon. To understand this is to begin to understand the significance of Matthew 1:1 (especially in the NRSV translation) which states that Jesus was a descendant of David! In Jesus the Messiah, the Davidic dynasty was being restored—but in a form very different from what the people were expecting! **Jesus, David's Final Descendant, washed feet, and calls His followers to do the same,** John 13:1–17, 31–35.

Individual Sins

The prophets passionately proclaimed that God's judgment would soon overtake the nation (***gavel*** on ***symbol for God***). The people were destroying themselves, the community, and the nation through sins such as those depicted in **ILLUSTRATION 22** and numbered below.

Gluttony and drunkenness: The order of the day was to consume food and ***drink***, rather than to show compassion for people in need, Hosea 7:5; Amos 4:1.

Self-pampering: The rich and the powerful sought the best of ***clothing and jewelry*** for themselves, but cared little about the plight of the needy, Isaiah 3:16–23; Ezekiel 16:48,49.

Ignorance and indifference: Few cared about the Word of the Lord, and were indifferent toward ***God's covenant*** (*shown broken*) with them, Hosea 4:4–6; 8:12; Isaiah 29:13; 30:9,10. They knew little about God's Word (***scrolls covered with cobwebs***).

Money—not mission: Many "professional prophets" opened their ***mouth*** only if they were paid well (***dollar sign***). They cared about their salaries but not about the welfare of their hearers, Micah 3:5,11; Jeremiah 6:13,14; 14:18.

Dishonesty: Scales and balances were rigged to enable the seller to cheat the buyer, Leviticus 19:35–37; Micah 6:9–12; Amos 8:4–6. The name of the game was "small measure, big price."

Corruption: Courts were corrupt, and many judges wielded the ***gavel*** in favor of those who paid them the biggest fee or bribe (***dollar sign***), Micah 3:1–3, 9–11.

Few took the prophetic attack seriously, Ezekiel 33:30–33. The people had lost their ability to blush, Jeremiah 6:13–15a. God's people were out-sinning Sodom and Gomorrah, Ezekiel 16:44–52. They could tell *rational lies* to *rationalize* anything!

ILLUSTRATION 23

National Sins

ILLUSTRATION 23 depicts the behavior patterns of the Israelites and the fate that God said would soon overtake them.

The People's Indifference to God's Will

The people did not look to God for national security or moral guidance.

- They trusted in the ***fortresses*** they had built, and in the ***weapons*** (***swords***) they had made to protect themselves, Hosea 8:14; Amos 2:5; Micah 5:10,11 (*top left*).
- Like a silly, senseless ***dove*** (*left center*), they fluttered from nation to nation to make ***alliances***, Hosea 7:11 (*top right*).
- The powerful exploited the weak, and used their ill-gotten gains to build themselves ***large houses of hewn stones*** surrounded by ***pleasant vineyards***, Amos 5:10,11 (*center*).

God's Discipline of a Rebellious People

God knew what His people were doing. God would soon demonstrate that though the people took His covenant lightly, He did not. He would let the "covenant curses" (Deuteronomy 28:15–68) come into effect in order to get His people's attention and to draw them back to Himself.

- God's people were fluttering around like senseless doves trying to make alliances with neighboring nations. God would put an end to all this. He would tear those senseless doves out of the air with His ***net*** (*left, center*, Hosea 7:12). He would permit their so-called "new friends" to swallow them up, Hosea 8:8.
- God's people had forgotten how good God had been to them—for example, how He had cared for and fed them during their time in the wilderness. The tragic truth was that, after they settled in Canaan, they soon had full bellies and empty memories! To restore them to their senses, God would soon stalk them like a leopard and maul them, Hosea 13:4–8 (***leopard creeping through grass, milepost behind it**, right*; the milepost signifies the long journeys the Israelites made to other nations to make alliances with them).
- To regain the attention of His distracted people, God would:
  a. flatten their ***fortresses***, smash their ***weapons***, and shred their ***alliances*** (*top, left to right*),
  b. tear down their ***houses*** and tear up their ***vineyards*** (*center*),
  c. reduce everything to ***rubble***, Zephaniah 1:13 (*bottom section*). Their fortresses and houses would soon disappear under ***nettles*** and ***thorns***, Hosea 9:6.

The people turned a deaf ear to the prophetic attack, insisting that God would not disturb the comfortable lifestyle they had chosen for themselves, Zephaniah 1:12b; Ezekiel 12:21–28.

But the people were wrong! God did intervene—to get their eyes off earthly things and to open their ears to His word and will.

- In 721 B.C., God permitted the Assyrians to devastate the Northern Kingdom of Israel and lead thousands of its citizens into exile, Micah 1:6.
- In 597 and 587 B.C., God permitted the Babylonians (under Nebuchadnezzar, His *servant*, Jeremiah 27:6) to devastate and discipline the Southern Kingdom and lead vast numbers of its citizens into exile in Babylon, 2 Kings 24:10–25:21.

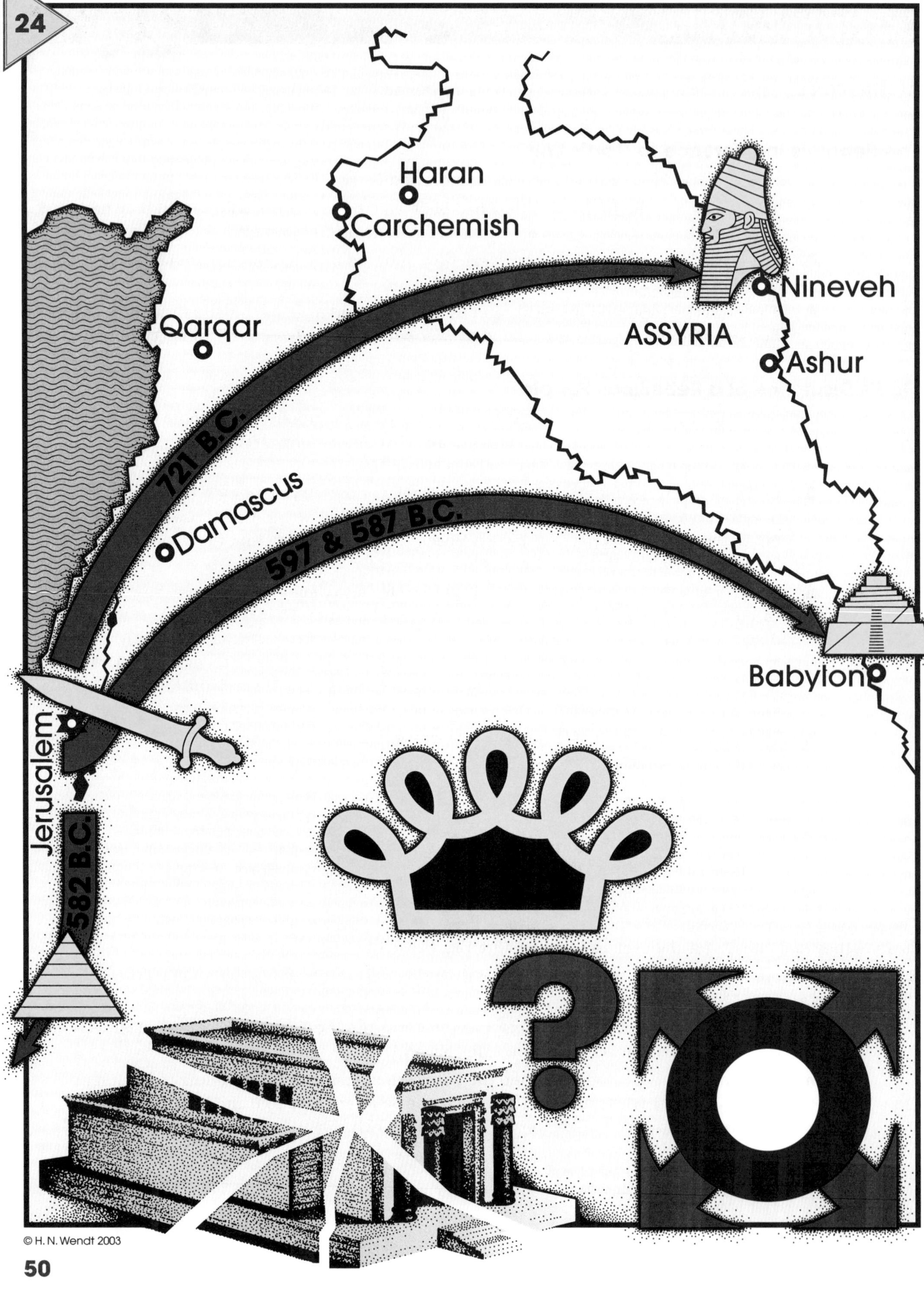

Haran
Carchemish
Nineveh
ASSYRIA
Ashur
Qarqar
721 B.C.
Damascus
597 & 587 B.C.
Babylon
Jerusalem
582 B.C.
?

The Prophetic Attack

The prophetic books constitute one-third of the Old Testament, or one-quarter of the Bible. They empower people today to hear, in astonishing ways, the passionate proclamations of those to whom the Lord revealed His truth and will. To understand the message and mission of Jesus the Messiah, we must understand the ministry of Israel's ancient prophets. After all, Jesus was that expected **Final Prophet**, Deut.18:15; Mark 9:7.

The Prophet's Role

Events within Israel and Judah did not go unnoticed. God raised up prophets to watch the ways of His people and to proclaim His Word and truth—no matter what the cost might be for the prophet. God would hold accountable those who proclaimed what the *people* wanted to hear rather than what *God* wanted the people to hear, Ezekiel 3:16–21.

The prophets (**ILLUSTRATION 21**, *bottom center*) began their message with statements such as, "Thus says the Lord," Amos 1:3; "Hear this word," Amos 3:1. Although on occasion the prophets predicted *future events* (Isaiah 60:1–61:6), they usually spoke about the *present situation*, Micah 3:1–12.

The Prophetic Message

The point of departure, the backdrop, for the prophetic attack was ***the covenant God made with His people at Sinai*** (**ILLUSTRATION 21**, *bottom right*). The prophets reminded the people who their God was, how good God had been to them, and how God's people were to live.

However, the prophets also proclaimed that because the people had repeatedly, and without remorse, broken the stipulations of the Sinai covenant (***broken tablet***), the covenant curses would come into effect. God Himself would soon lead the armies of surrounding nations against His own people (***swords on arrows pointing to Palestine from surrounding nations***).

- ***Assyrian king*** (*top right*)***:*** God would use the Assyrians as a club to vent His anger against His people. When the Assyrian forces used clubs to beat them, those clubs would express God's fury against an indifferent and rebellious people, Isaiah 10:5.
- ***Babylonian temple*** (*center right*)***:*** God would use Nebuchadnezzar, King of Babylon, as His servant to punish and discipline a people who cared nothing for God's Word and will, Jeremiah 27:6.
- ***Egyptian pyramid*** (*bottom left*)***:*** The Egyptian armies would march north, city by city, to attack God's indifferent people, Micah 1:10–16. For each village name, Micah used a play on words to describe what would eventually overtake God's people. For example, "Gath" means *winepress*. In Gath, where wine flowed forth, no tears would flow forth; the people would be so grief-stricken that they would not be able to weep.

The prophets often used fiery language, Jeremiah 4:5–31. On occasion, they acted out their messages, Ezekiel chs. 4,5. Their ministries were often anything but easy, Jeremiah 20:7–18.

Few people took the prophets seriously, they felt no shame about their sinful ways (Jeremiah 6:13–15a), and cared little for God's covenant with them. They felt that they were politically and materially secure because they were a *special people*, living in a *special land*, worshiping a *special God* who lived in a *special house* in a *special city!* Some harassed and even killed the prophets, Jeremiah 20:1,2; 26:23.

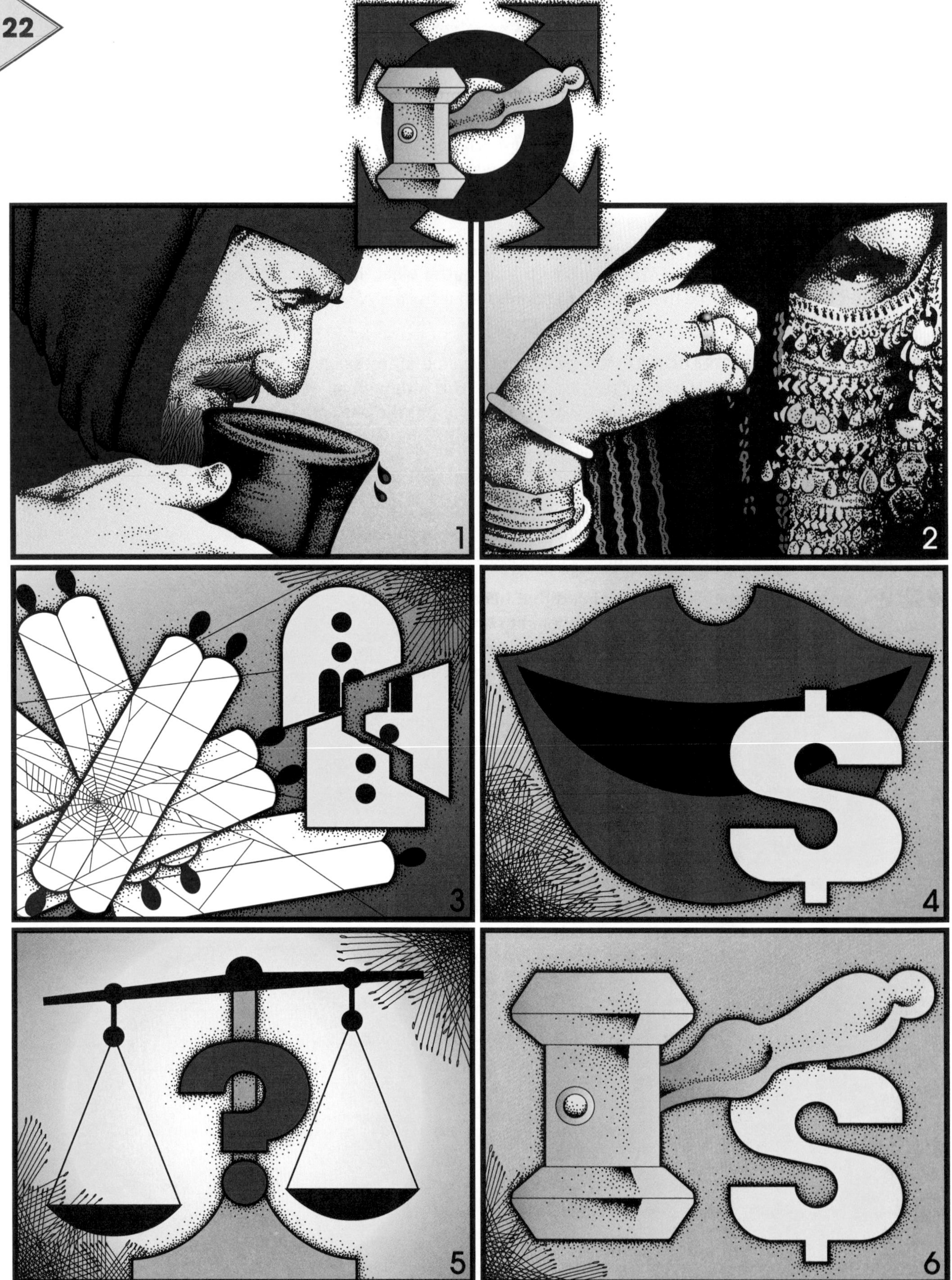
1
2
3
4
5
6

End and Exile

 Israel's History Comes to an End

a. **ILLUSTRATION 24**, ***upper arrow from Northern Kingdom to Assyria***; ***head of an Assyrian king:*** The Assyrians destroyed the Northern Kingdom in ***721 B.C.*** and scattered many of its citizens around their vast empire, 2 Kings 17. They also resettled people from their own realm within the devastated Northern Kingdom. Many of these intermarried with Israelites the Assyrians had left behind. The offspring of these unions were known as Samaritans—a name derived from Samaria, the former capital of the Northern Kingdom.

b. The Samaritans accepted the *Torah* (Pentateuch, or Genesis–Deuteronomy) as their sacred writings, and worshiped one God at one place—Gerizim, John 4:20,21. They insisted that Deuteronomy's frequent references to "the place where the Lord would make His name to dwell" (e.g., ch. 12) had to do with Mt. Gerizim, not Jerusalem, and that when Abraham was preparing to sacrifice Isaac on a mountain, that mountain was Mt. Gerizim—not Mt. Zion in Jerusalem. Still today, Mt. Gerizim is the Samaritan's "holy mountain." It is located just south of what in biblical times was called Shechem, but today is called Nablus.

 Judah Goes into Exile

a. ***Arrow from Southern Kingdom to Babylon***; ***Babylonian temple:*** Assyrian control over Judah remained firm until about 630 B.C., but then began to weaken. After a brief period under the Egyptians (609–605 B.C), Judah came under Babylonian control.

b. King Jehoiakim (598 B.C.) and later King Zedekiah (588 B.C.) revolted against the Babylonians—who responded swiftly. They put down the first revolt, and, after the second, devastated the land, Jerusalem, and the Temple. In 597 and 587 B.C. they led many from Judah into exile—including King Jehoiachin (Jehoiakim's son and successor) and King Zedekiah. When in ***582 B.C.*** rebels in Judah killed the (Jewish) governor appointed by the Babylonians, ***many in Judah fled to Egypt*** (2 Kings 25:22–26), taking with them the prophet Jeremiah and his scribe Baruch, Jeremiah chs. 43, 44.

c. Jehoiachin was only 18 years of age when taken to Babylon in 597 B.C. Many hoped he would live through the exile, return to Jerusalem, and reestablish the Davidic dynasty (he was still alive in 560 B.C., 2 Kings 25:27–30). However, both Jehoiachin and Zedekiah died in Babylon.

3 The Exiles Taken to Babylon Ask Soul-Searching Questions

a. ***Crown:*** What would God do about His covenant with David? Many hoped that one day the Davidic dynasty would be restored, Psalm 89.

b. ***Shattered Temple:*** Was Israel's history in relation to the Promised Land, Jerusalem, and the Temple to come to an end?

c. ***Symbol for God:*** Did God really exist? Did God really care about Israel? Should the Israelites forsake the God they had worshiped in Jerusalem, and worship the Babylonian gods? After all, there were many large temples in Babylon!

Many concluded that they deserved the disaster that had overtaken them, for they had refused to listen to the prophets!

ILLUSTRATION 25

Judah, You are Going Home!

Upper section

Creation 1 and ***Exodus 1***

Sometime during the years preceding 539 B.C., prophets told the exiles in Babylon that God was about to rescue them and restore them to the Promised Land. In proclaiming that *good news* (or *gospel*, Isaiah 60:1–4), the prophets used terminology reflecting God's actions in creating the universe and in the first Exodus.

Lower section

Creation 2 and ***Exodus 2***

Some of the points God makes in Isaiah chs. 40–66 are:

- "As I once opened the waters to rescue you from bondage in Egypt, so I will open the waters to rescue you from Babylon," 43:14–21 (***open chains***, ***parted water***).
- "I will build a highway back through the wilderness from Babylon to Jerusalem. Your journey will be comfortable and quick!" 40:3–5 (***arrow from Babylon to Jerusalem***).
- "The Babylonian gods will not intervene. They cannot! They are nothings, made out of wood," 40:18–20; 44:14–19 (***Babylonian ziggurat, or temple***).
- "I, your King, will lead you back like a gentle, tender shepherd," 40:9–11 (***crown***). "I will go in front of you to guide you, and behind you to protect you—just as I did when I rescued you from Egypt," 52:12 (***pillars of fire and cloud***).
- "The journey back through the wilderness will be very different from the journey you made when you left Egypt. This time I will ensure that there is plenty of water and shade," 41:17–20 (***trees and stream***).
- "The land to which you are returning will be like a new Eden, a veritable Paradise," 51:1–3 (***God's creating hand over the Promised Land***).
- "You will sing hymns of praise all the way as I lead you back, and Jerusalem will welcome us home with shouts of joy," 40:9–11; 51:11 (***figures with raised hands***).

However, those who returned to Judah were disillusioned. They went back expecting to find the Messianic Age, but found only a mess! Jerusalem was little more than a pile of rubble. Nothing had changed since the Babylonian devastation of 587 B.C.

26

613

Once to Babylon is Enough!

Many of the exiles finally realized that they deserved the disaster that had overtaken them. They had turned their backs on God and His covenant. What must they do to ensure that a similar catastrophe would not overtake them again?

 ***Crown*** and ***question mark*** (**ILLUSTRATION 26**, *top center*)***:*** The Davidic dynasty was apparently at an end. Would God ever restore it?

 ***Symbol for God***, ***Temple***, ***people around the Temple*** (*center*)***:*** Though the people no longer had an earthly king, they did have a King—God Himself. God's special "house" was the Jerusalem Temple—and the priests made God's mercy and will known to the people. The community of Israel must honor and worship God in a fitting manner, and offer sacrifice in only one place—the Jerusalem Temple. (The "one place" referred to in Deuteronomy 12:5,11,14,18,21,26, 14:23,24,25, 15:20, 16:2,6,7,11,15,16, 17:8,10, 18: 6 was eventually interpreted to mean "Jerusalem," 2 Kings chs. 22,23; see also 1 Chron. 11–2 Chron. 9.) No more idolatry!

 ***Scrolls*** (*top left*)***:*** The preexilic community had ignored the proclamations of the prophets. The postexilic community must study their sacred writings—writings that revealed God's undeserved mercy and gracious will. They must understand the reasons the prophets gave for the doom that had overtaken the nation, and learn from them! (See again **ILLUSTRATIONS 21**, **22**, and **23**.) The exile had been a painful experience.

 ***Large and small law-codes*** (*top left*)***:*** The people must know God's will—*in detail*. Therefore the scribes studied and taught not only the ***613 law-codes*** in "Moses' writings" (words, they insisted, that God had dictated to Moses on Sinai and which Moses had written), but also the "oral traditions" (***small law tablets around the large law tablet***) which, they said, God had whispered to Moses at Sinai and which had to be handed down to successive generations in memorized form. The goal of the oral traditions was to relate ancient commandments to new situations.

 ***Small Covenant—large law code symbols*** (*top right*)***:*** As time went by, the teachers emphasized obedience so much that it overshadowed their understanding of covenant and grace. Many people thought that, through obedience, they could manipulate God. Many saw the law codes as a merit system. If they were obedient, they would never again suffer calamities such as the Babylonian exile (***question mark***, ***a***nd ***arrow pointing backward***). Furthermore, obedience would encourage God to send their Messiah (***question mark***, and ***arrow pointing forward***).

 ***Circles around Judah*** (*bottom left*)***:*** Some stressed that God had formed them as a people to make Him known to surrounding nations, Isaiah 2:2–4; Micah 4:1–4.

 ***Servant figure*** (*bottom right*) and ***lamp with red flame*** (*center*)***:*** The people were to be a light to the nations by teaching others about their God and living as a servant community, Isaiah 49:1–6.

Those who began returning to *Judah* in 538 B.C. were the first to be called *Jews*. From them grew that system of belief today referred to as *Judaism*. It placed much emphasis on knowing, understanding, and living according to the Law, the first five books of the Old Testament, the *Torah*.

ILLUSTRATION 27

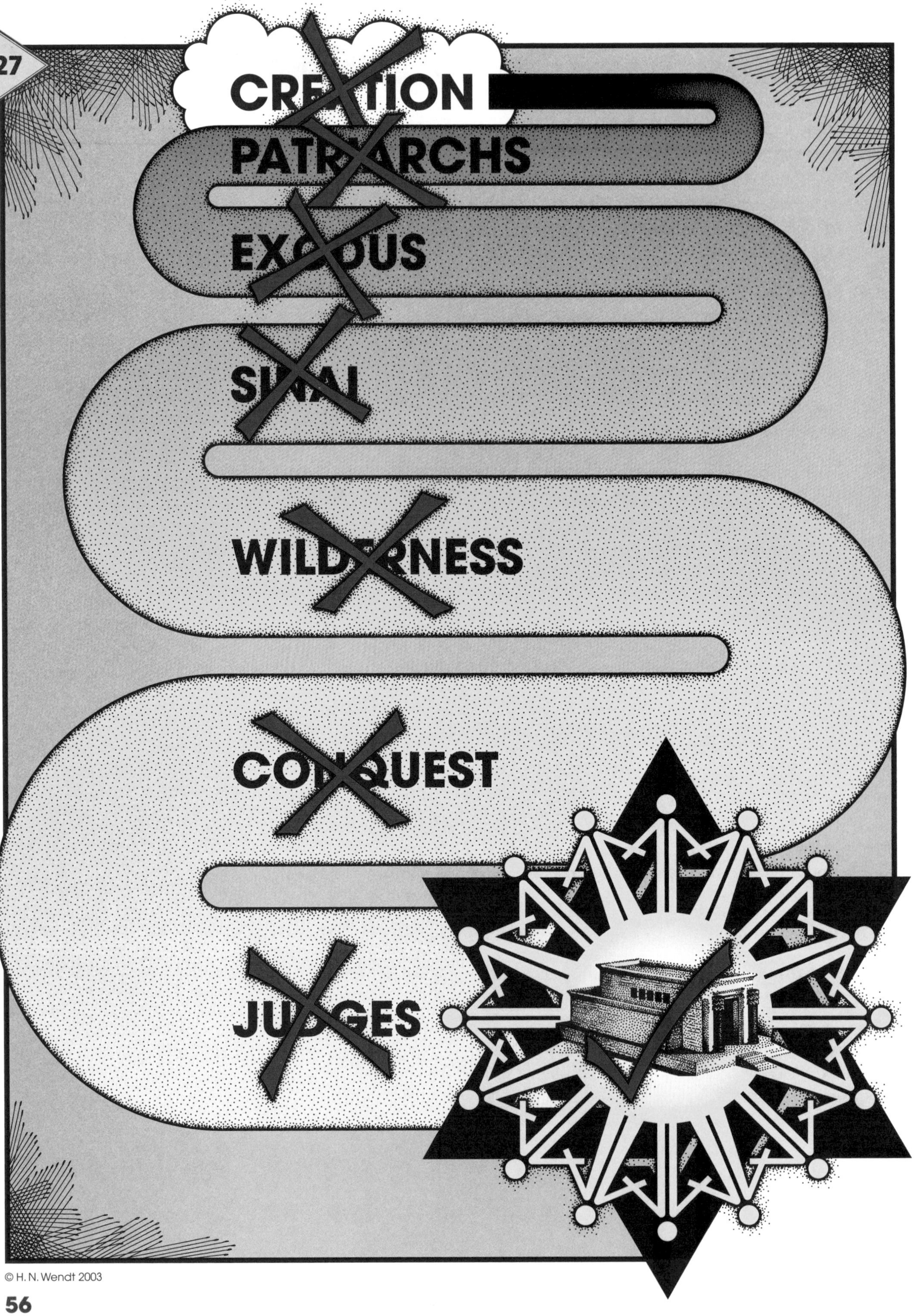

CREATION

PATRIARCHS

EXODUS

SINAI

WILDERNESS

CONQUEST

JUDGES

Behold, Judaism!

 1 and 2 Chronicles present a "second history" of God's people that begins in earnest in 1 Chron. 10 with an account of Saul's death. The first nine chapters list only names and genealogies, and (as depicted in **ILLUSTRATION 27** by cancel symbol "***X***") omit all reference to:

- ***CREATION***
- the period of the ***PATRIARCHS*** (Abraham, Isaac, Jacob)
- the ***EXODUS*** from Egypt
- the events at ***SINAI***
- the ***WILDERNESS*** period
- the ***CONQUEST***
- the ***JUDGES***
- Saul's reign
- David's early life.

 The Chronicler's "saintly" David (***star of David***, *bottom right*) devoted most of his reign to planning the ***Jerusalem Temple*** (*bottom right*) and producing music and liturgies for use in its worship life, 1 Chron. chs 11–29. The Chronicler's "saintly" Solomon built the ***Temple*** (2 Chron. chs. 1–9), which now became the focal point of Judah's history and all history, and the reason for the nation's existence (***approval mark on Temple***, ***circle of people around Temple***).

 1 and 2 Chronicles refer to the history of the former Northern Kingdom only when that was necessary for making sense out of Judah's history. The writers suggest that the Northern Kingdom never really belonged to God; it did not submit to the Davidic dynasty and did not acknowledge Jerusalem as God's dwelling place or worship at its Temple. *Judah was the true people of God, the true Israel! Jerusalem was the only legitimate place for offering sacrifice!*

 The following opinions became increasingly established:

- *God's special people*, Israel, consisted of the tribe of Judah.
- *God's special land* was the land of Judah.
- *God's special city* was Jerusalem.
- *God's special dwelling place* was the Jerusalem Temple.
- *The special link between God and His people* was the *Torah*, the Old Testament writings (in particular, the *Pentateuch*—Genesis through Deuteronomy).

 Though not depicted in **ILLUSTRATION 27**, the books known as Ezra and Nehemiah report the following:

a. From 538 B.C. onward, groups of exiles undertook the long journey back to Judah and Jerusalem. Soon after their return, they set up an altar, restored some traditional worship rituals, and in 515 B.C. dedicated a new Temple—about which little is known.

b. Later, Nehemiah, a Jewish official serving in the Persian court, returned to Jerusalem and organized the rebuilding of the city's walls. A little later Ezra, a priest, taught the people about their law codes and the covenant.

c. Both Nehemiah and Ezra were disturbed that many Jewish men were marrying Gentile women. Nehemiah forbade such marriages. Ezra insisted that those which had already taken place be dissolved. The goal was to keep the Jewish religion pure by keeping the nation pure. (After all, Solomon's many foreign wives had brought with them many foreign gods!) People came to believe that to be a Jew was automatically to belong to God. The point of entry into the people of God was the womb of a Jewish mother!

ILLUSTRATION 28

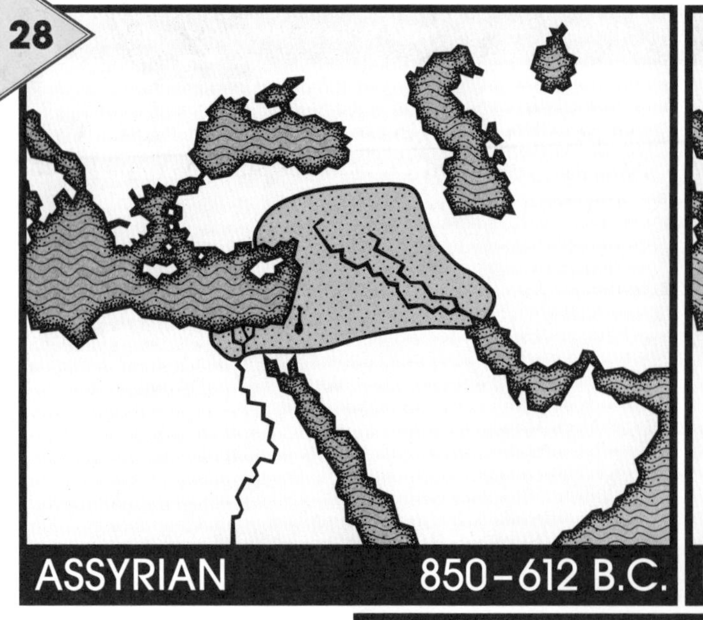

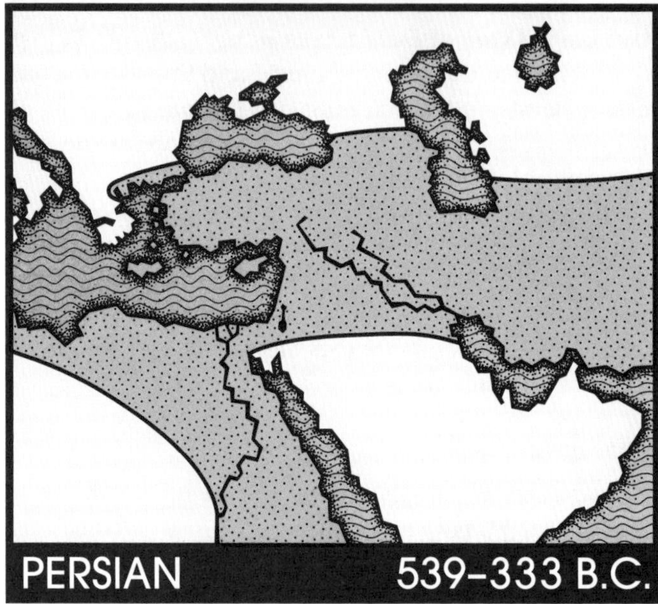

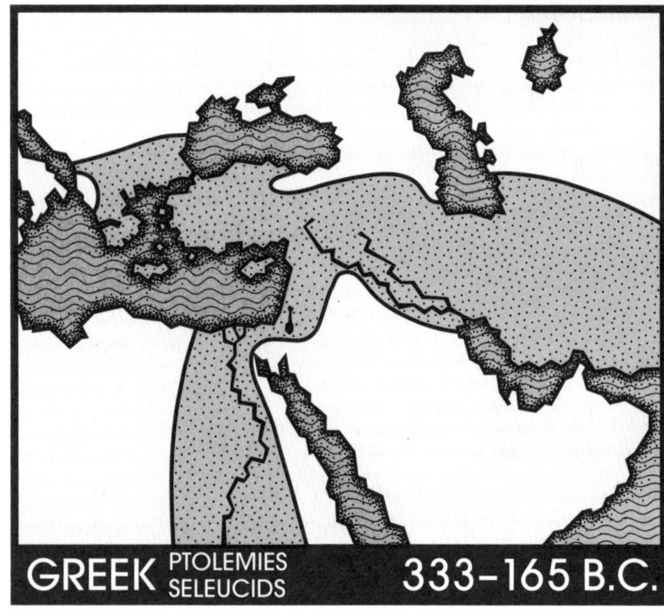

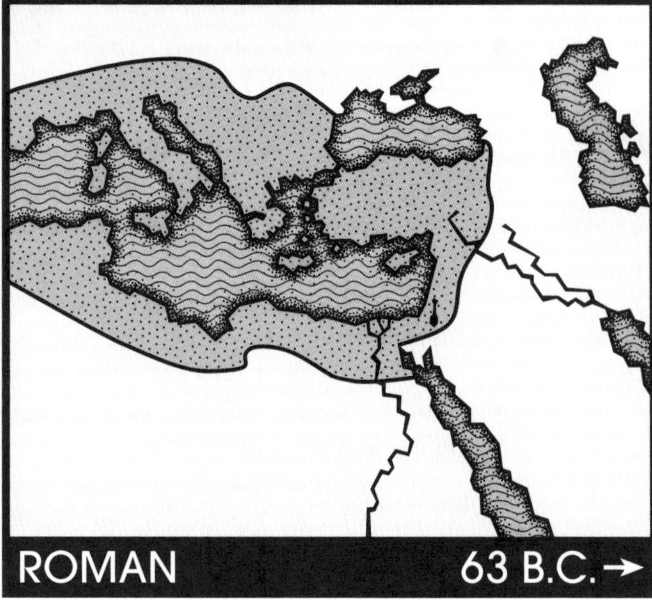

Memories and Hopes

The maps in **ILLUSTRATION 28** depict the five empires that played a key role in the history of ancient Israel. One empire after another took control of Israel and made it part of its empire. The illustration does not depict the roles that Egypt and Syria played in Israel's history.

The Assyrian Empire

Assyria was politically at work in the Middle East region even before the time of the patriarchs. Fortunately for Israel, Assyrian influence was at its lowest point during the reign of Israel's most popular king, David (1,000–960 B.C.). In due course, Assyria's power increased, and its influence—particularly in the Northern Kingdom of Israel—resulted in that Kingdom becoming an Assyrian vassal in 841 B.C. As Assyria's fortunes and power decreased, Israel and Judah gained some freedom and prominence under Jeroboam II and Uzziah. However, in 745 B.C., Tiglath-Pileser III set about restoring Assyria's imperial state, and dealt harshly with Israelite attempts to gain independence. In 721 B.C., the Assyrians overran the Northern Kingdom of Israel, led its people into exile, and brought Israel's history to an end.

The Babylonian Empire

The best-known king of the First Babylonian Dynasty (18th century B.C., about the time of Abraham) was Hammurabi, the author of a famous code of laws. During the early part of the first millennium B.C., the Assyrians controlled Babylon. However, the Babylonians finally threw off the Assyrian yoke in 612 B.C., and then dominated the history of Western Asia until 539 B.C. Nebuchadnezzar led the Southern Kingdom of Judah into exile in Babylon via two deportations in 597 and 587 B.C.

The Persian Empire

The Persians under Cyrus conquered the Babylonians in 539 B.C., and then went on to develop and control an empire stretching from India to the Aegean Sea and Egypt. The Persian rulers treated captive nations much more kindly than did the Assyrians and the Babylonians. Eventually their realm became part of the empire of Alexander the Great.

The Greek Empire

After Philip of Macedon was assassinated in 336 B.C., his son Alexander, then only 20 years old, succeeded him. By the time of his death in 323 B.C. at the age of 33, Alexander the Great had conquered much of the Mediterranean world. He died during a campaign in Babylon, but before his death he divided the empire among his generals.

Two generals are of particular interest in the history of the Jews: Ptolemy and Seleucus. Ptolemy and his descendants (the *Ptolemies*) gained control of Egypt (and ruled Jewish territory 301–198 B.C.). Seleucus and his descendants (the *Seleucids*) ruled Syria—and gained control of Jewish territory in 198 B.C. The Jews, under the leadership of the Maccabees, began a struggle for freedom from the Seleucids in 165 B.C.—and finally won full independence in 142 B.C. The Maccabees established a line of Jewish kings known as the Hasmoneans. The Hasmoneans were not descendants of David.

The Roman Empire

In 63 B.C., Pompey made Syria (which included Judah) a Roman province. With that move, the Jewish people came under Roman domination for several centuries.

In Jesus' day, the Jews looked for a coming Messiah to deliver them from the Romans. However, the New Testament writers point out that the Romans did not constitute the "real enemy," Matthew 1:21.

ILLUSTRATION 29

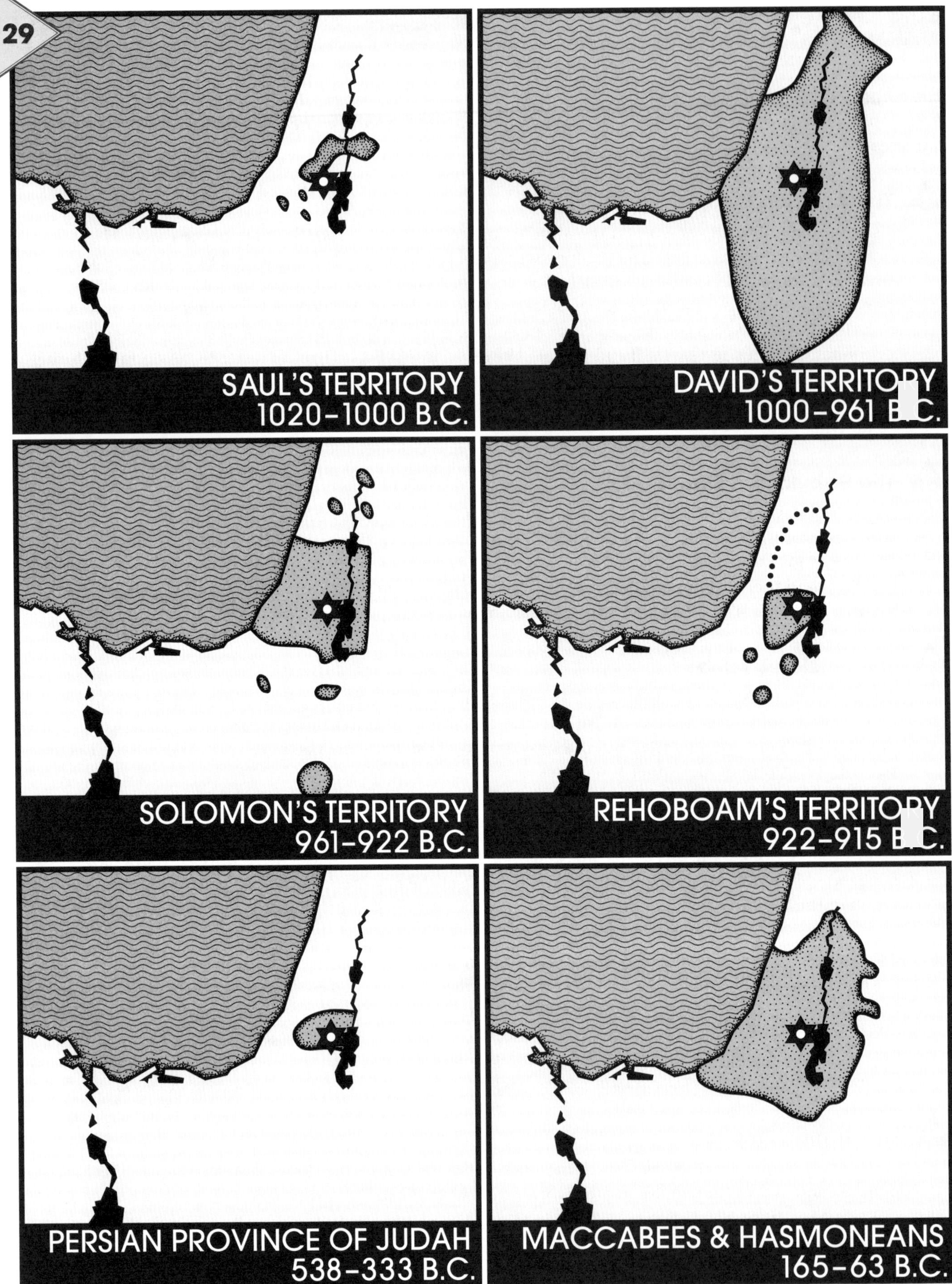

Memories and Dreams

ILLUSTRATION 29 shows how the nation's borders increased and decreased as its fortunes waxed and waned. The postexilic community hoped that God would one day make their realm as large as David's kingdom had been.

Saul's Territory

The size of the realm Saul ruled is uncertain. Though many believe that Saul's kingdom was quite small (as frame 1 depicts), 1 Samuel 14:47,48 suggests that Saul captured and controlled a realm as large as that which David later ruled.

David's Territory

David's realm was large. The memory of what it had once been continued to influence the Jewish people throughout their history and gave rise to the Zealot revolts against the Romans in A.D. 66–70 and 132–135.

Solomon's Territory

There are suggestions that Solomon's realm was even larger than David's, 1 Kings 4:21. However, towards the close of Solomon's reign, his realm decreased in size when the Syrians and Edomites gained their independence, 1 Kings 11:14–25.

Rehoboam's Territory

Solomon's son, Rehoboam, gained control only of Judah. The Northern Kingdom was taken over by Jeroboam and ruled by nine different dynasties; it was destroyed by the Assyrians in 721 B.C. After revolts against Babylon by King Jehoiakim and King Zedekiah, many from Judah were taken into exile in Babylon in 597 and 587 B.C. In 538 B.C., some of the exiles in Babylon began to return to Judah.

Persian Province of Judah

Postexilic Judah was small, and apart from a short period under the Maccabees and their descendants, the Hasmoneans, it was never free.

Maccabees & Hasmoneans

The Maccabees revolted against the Syrians in 165 B.C., and finally gained full independence in 142 B.C. Their descendants, the Hasmoneans, eventually established a realm of considerable size. Some viewed their realm as the messianic kingdom. Although the Maccabees-Hasmoneans were Levites, they were not descendants of Zadok—a factor which angered many when the Hasmoneans assumed the role of High Priest. (Here note 1 Kings 1:38 and 1 Chron. 15:11, and the frequent references to Zadok that follow in 1 and 2 Chronicles.) The level of anger increased even more when the Hasmoneans combined the role of High Priest with that of king. *Only descendants of David could be considered legitimate kings!* In 63 B.C., the Romans took control of Judah.

For hundreds of years, many within Judaism hoped that one day God would restore the Davidic kingdom. Up to the very moment of Jesus' ascension, even Jesus' disciples shared that hope, Acts 1:6.

ILLUSTRATION 30

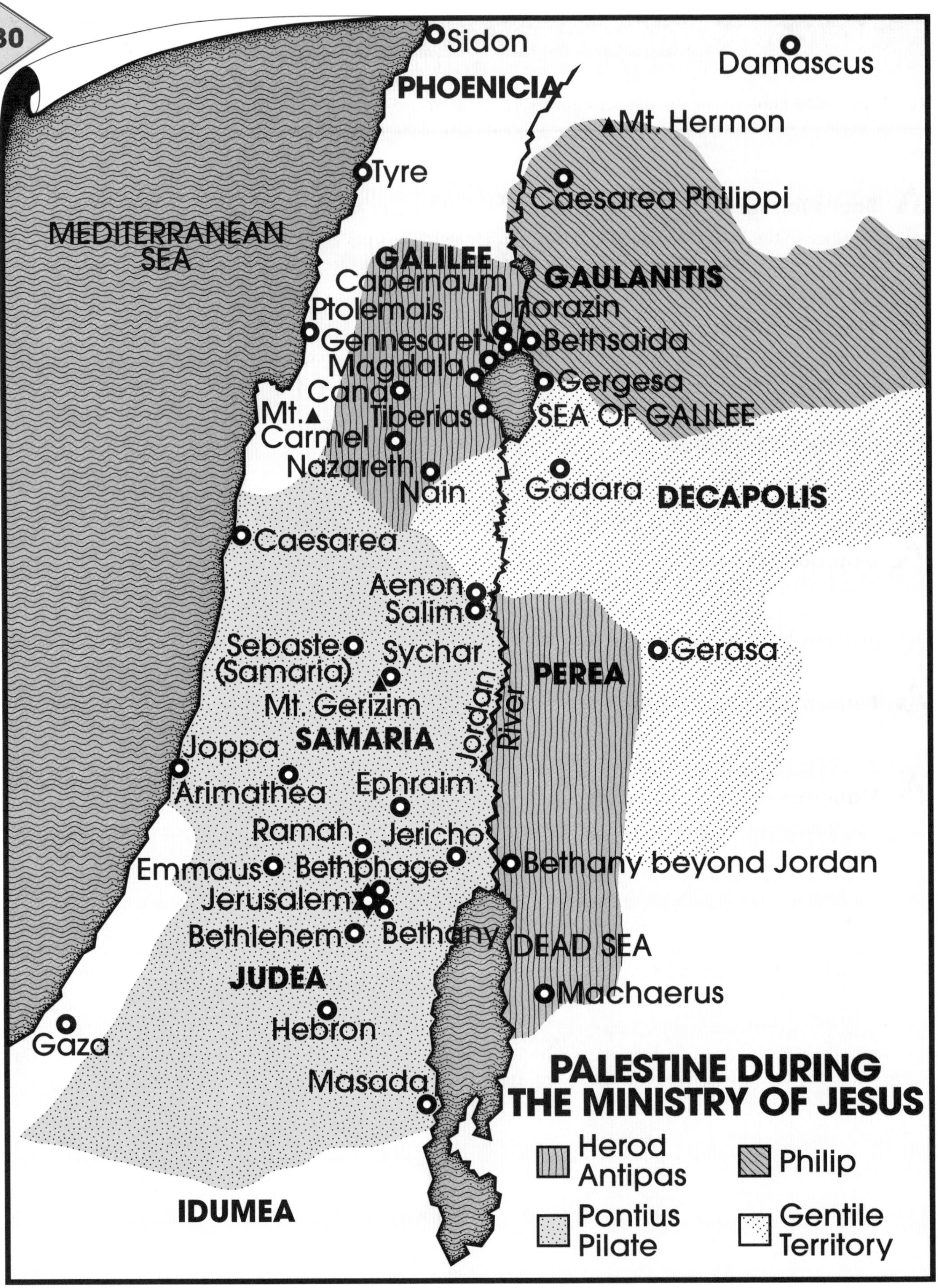

PALESTINE DURING THE MINISTRY OF JESUS

Herod Antipas
Philip
Pontius Pilate
Gentile Territory

Sidon
Damascus
PHOENICIA
Mt. Hermon
Tyre
Caesarea Philippi
MEDITERRANEAN SEA
GALILEE
Capernaum
GAULANITIS
Ptolemais
Chorazin
Gennesaret
Bethsaida
Magdala
Cana
Gergesa
Mt. Carmel
Tiberias
SEA OF GALILEE
Nazareth
Nain
Gadara
DECAPOLIS
Caesarea
Aenon
Salim
Sebaste (Samaria)
Sychar
Gerasa
Mt. Gerizim
PEREA
Jordan River
Joppa
SAMARIA
Arimathea
Ephraim
Ramah
Jericho
Emmaus
Bethphage
Bethany beyond Jordan
Jerusalem
Bethlehem
Bethany
DEAD SEA
JUDEA
Machaerus
Gaza
Hebron
Masada
IDUMEA

The Stage for Jesus' Ministry

ILLUSTRATION 30 contains information about the locations and geographical areas that played a role in the Gospel accounts of Jesus' ministry.

 Herod the Great came to power, with Roman help, in 37 B.C. In the second decade of his reign, Herod expanded his kingdom to the north and into the territory east of the ***Jordan River*** (usually referred to as "the Transjordan"). He enlarged the city of Samaria (called ***Sebaste***, Greek for Augustus) and built in it a temple to Caesar Augustus. He erected a great palace on the western side of Mt. Zion in ***Jerusalem***, surrounded by elevated gardens and courts, and flanked by three huge towers. This complex served as the seat of government for Herod, and was later used by Roman procurators when they visited Jerusalem from ***Caesarea***. (It is possible that the *praetorium* in which Pilate tried Jesus was located in this complex.) Herod also built a number of palaces, including lavish ones at ***Jericho*** and ***Masada***. He built the city of Caesarea on the Mediterranean coast, complete with an artificial harbor surrounded by huge breakwaters and towers.

 After Herod the Great died in 4 B.C., his realm was divided among his three sons: Archelaeus, Herod Antipas, and Philip.

a. Archelaeus ruled ***Judea*** and ***Samaria*** until A.D. 6, when he was disgraced, deposed, and deported by the Romans. After this, Roman prefects and procurators (e.g. Pontius Pilate) ruled these territories.

b. Herod Antipas ruled ***Galilee*** and ***Perea***.

c. Philip ruled the region of ***Gaulanitis*** (today, the Golan Heights).

 The ***Decapolis*** (Greek for "Ten Towns"), which consisted of a number of independent cities, did not come under Jewish control. It is important to note that the people Jesus encountered when visiting the Decapolis seemed to understand more about His person than did His own people.

a. When, in the Decapolis, he encountered a man possessed with demons, the man called out, "Jesus, Son of the Most High God," Mark 5:7.

b. The man in the Decapolis to whom Jesus gave the ability to hear and speak gave fervent witness to Jesus, Mark 7:31–37.

c. After feeding 4,000 Gentiles (non-Jews) in the Decapolis (Mark 8:1–10; see 7:31), there were *seven* baskets of left-overs. Deuteronomy 7:1 and other Old Testament passages refer to *seven* nations on Israel's borders that the people hated.

 When Jesus encountered a Gentile woman in ***Phoenicia*** (present-day Lebanon, west of Galilee), she addressed Him as "Lord, Son of David," Matthew 15:21,25,27. His own people never addressed Him in these terms during His earthly ministry.

 According to John 1:28, John the Baptist carried out his ministry at ***Bethany beyond the Jordan***—in the general area where the Israelites first the crossed the Jordan under Joshua; see Joshua 3. The Jewish historian, Josephus, wrote that Herod Antipas ordered John the Baptist beheaded in ***Machaerus***—a large fortress-palace.

 The Samaritans, whom the Jews hated, insisted that the only legitimate place for worship was the summit of ***Mt. Gerizim***. They said Abraham took Isaac there when responding to God's directive to sacrifice him, Genesis 22.

ILLUSTRATION 31

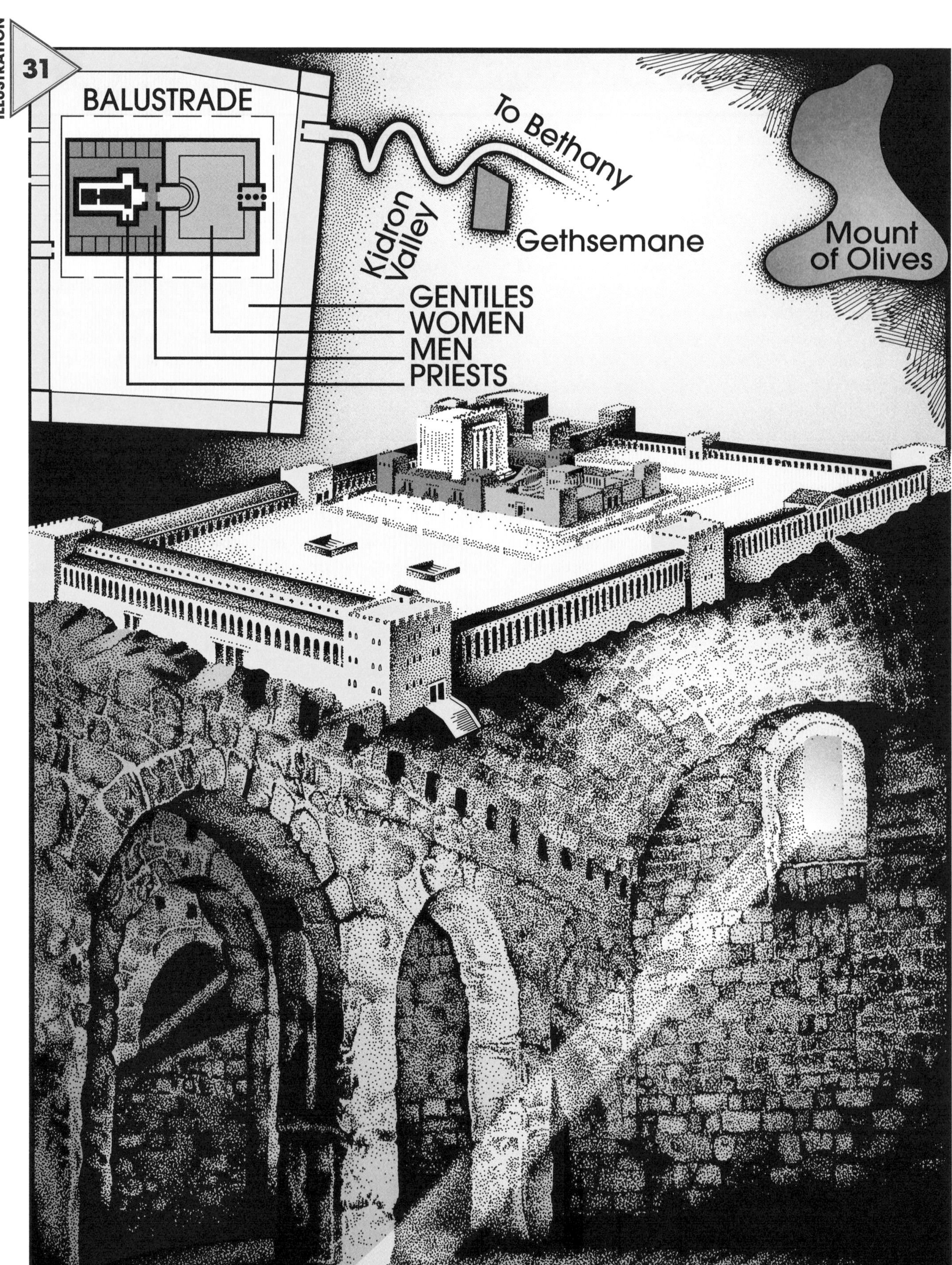

New Testament—Religious Background 1 31

WORSHIP CENTERS

The Temple

 Prior to 621 B.C., there were many shrines in Judah, just as there had been many in Israel prior to its destruction in 721 B.C. As a result of King Josiah's reform movement in 621 B.C. (2 Kings chs. 22, 23), worship was centralized in Jerusalem and all other shrines were destroyed. Eventually, facilities were provided in the Temple area for changing money and for selling animals to be used in sacrifice.

 Solomon's Temple was destroyed in 587 B.C. The postexilic Temple, dedicated in 515 B.C., was replaced by a grand structure (**ILLUSTRATION 31**) begun by Herod the Great in 19 B.C., completed about A.D. 63, but destroyed by the Romans in A.D. 70.

 Herod's Temple was huge. The southern *Royal Porch* was nearly 1,000 feet (320 meters) long, and contained 160 pillars in four rows of 40 pillars, each about 15 feet (5 meters) in circumference. The eastern *Solomon's Porch* was nearly 1,500 feet (480 meters) long. In the northwest corner of the Temple platform was the *Fortress of Antonia* where (possibly) Pilate tried Jesus.

- ▲ Worshipers gained access to the Temple by passing through the ***Huldah gates*** (*shown in the southern wall*), walking through ornate underground passage-ways, and then climbing stairs to reach the Temple platform (***stair openings*** *on platform surface*).
- ▲ Right of access to the Temple was determined by rank. Only the High Priest could enter the Temple's inner *Holy of Holies*, which he did one day each year; only ***priests*** could enter the *Holy Place*, and did so each day (here see **ILLUSTRATION 18**). Only Jewish ***men*** could enter the *Court of the Men*; only Jewish ***women*** could enter the *Court of the Women*.
- ▲ A low stone ***balustrade*** (called in Hebrew the *soreq*) surrounded the Temple itself. Its purpose was to limit access to the Temple. It contained 13 openings or entry points—***five in the southern wall***, ***three in the eastern wall***, and ***five in the northern wall.*** Only Jews (those *within* the covenant community) could pass through those gates to enter the area within the balustrade. ***Gentiles*** (those *outside* the covenant community) were forbidden to go beyond the balustrade; if they did, they were killed.
- ▲ Parts of the southeast section of the Temple platform were so high above ground level that they were supported by a series of ***columns and rooms with arched ceilings*** (depicted in *lower section* of **ILLUSTRATION 31**). The stones used in building the Temple were held together by gravity; no cement was used.

Synagogues (not depicted)

 Because many lived at some distance from Judea's one Temple in Jerusalem, each community had its own *synagogue*. The term is derived from a Greek word meaning "to come together"; hence, a synagogue is a *meeting place*.

 During Sabbath worship in the synagogues, a leader read and explained passages from the Law and the Prophets, and offered prayers. No sacrifices were offered. Men and women sat in different parts of the building.

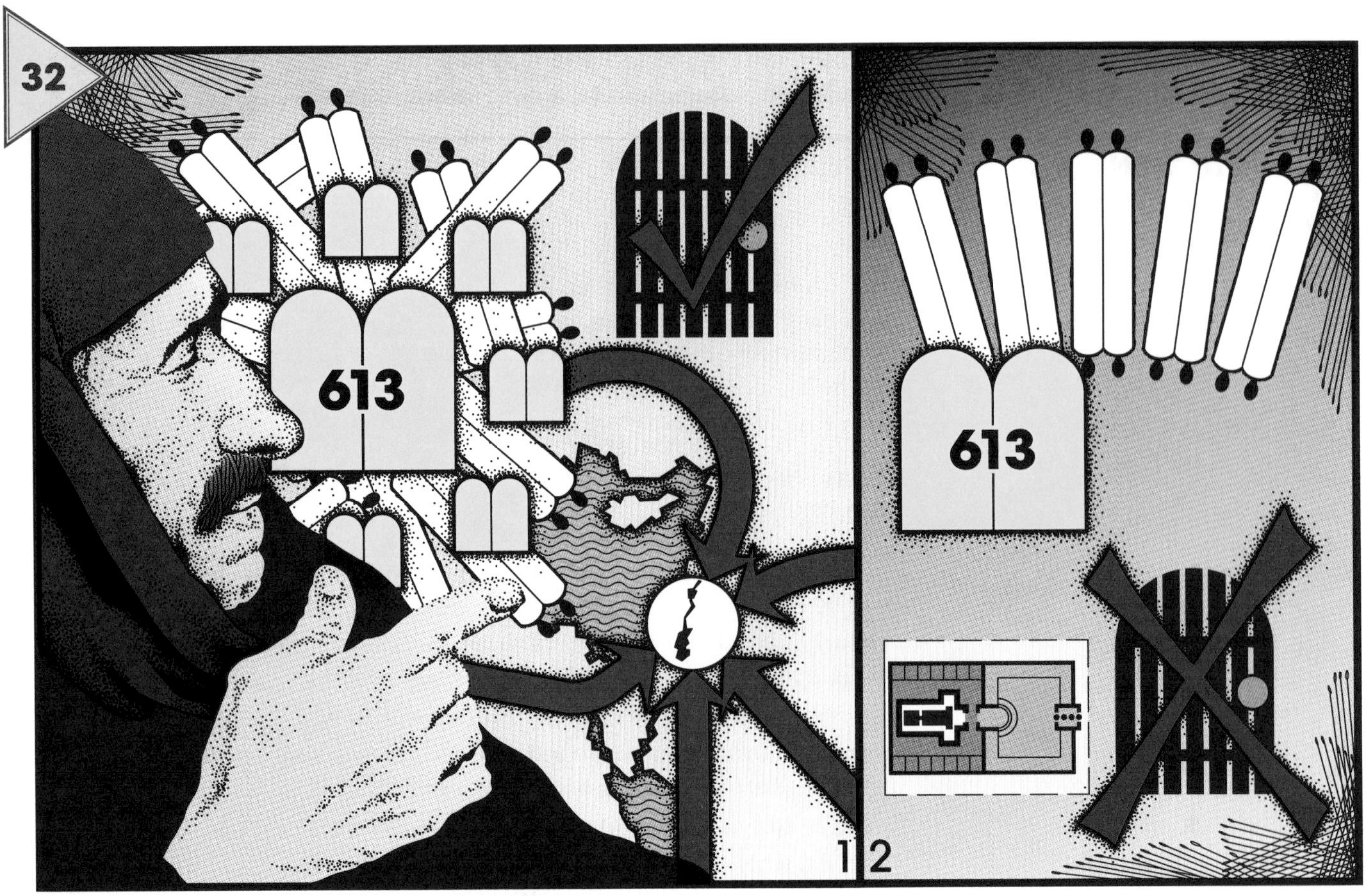

32

613

613

1 2

ONE GOD • NATIONALISM • TORAH(LAW)

3 4

New Testament—Religious Background 2 32

JUDAISM: BELIEFS AND PRACTICES

Major Groups within Judaism

Upper left

 The ***Pharisees*** accepted as authoritative the books in the Hebrew Scriptures (***scrolls***), all ***613 laws*** in the Pentateuch, and all the oral traditions (***small law tablets***). They said that when the Messianic Age broke in, it would take place in Judah (***circle around Judah***). Jews scattered around the Mediterranean world would return to Judah (***arrows pointing back to Judah***), and dead Jews would be resurrected to participate in that Age (***symbol for belief in resurrection: door with slats, and approval sign on it***).

Upper right

 The ***Sadducees*** accepted only the first five books in the Hebrew Scriptures (***five scrolls***) as authoritative, and concentrated on those sections dealing with worship and rituals in the Temple (***ground-plan***, *bottom left*). They accepted as authoritative the ***613 laws*** in the Pentateuch, but rejected the oral traditions of the scribes and Pharisees (small law tablets omitted from this section). They did not believe in angels and demons, or the resurrection of the body and immortality (***symbol for belief in resurrection canceled out***, *bottom right*).

Lower left

 The ***Scribes*** were students, interpreters, and teachers of the Law. They were also referred to as rabbis, or teachers. They devoted their lives to the study of the Law so that they might obtain wisdom (***lamp***). Eventually, in about A.D. 200, the teachings of the rabbis were collected and produced in written form in the *Mishnah*—and in later collections known as the *Gemara* and *Tosefta* (***scroll***; ***arrows point back from the teachings of the rabbis to the central biblical text***).

Lower right

 The ***Zealots*** urged the use of force (***sword***) to win freedom from Roman control (***Roman helmet***) and to usher in the Messianic Age.

Beliefs and Sects

- ***ONE GOD:*** Only one God existed—the God of the Jews. All other so-called "gods" were nothings.
- ***NATIONALISM:*** Only Jews belonged to this one God. Gentiles who wanted to belong to God had to embrace the Jewish faith, become Jews, and live as Jews.
- ***TORAH (LAW):*** The term "Torah" could be used for all the Hebrew Scriptures, or for the Pentateuch (the first Five Books), or for the law codes embedded within the Pentateuch. It could also be used to refer to the oral traditions. The Torah was the link between God and His people; to belong to God required conformity and obedience to the commandments in the Torah. The Torah was referred to as *the bread of life*, *the water of life*, and *the light of the world*.
- The ***Essenes*** (not depicted in **ILLUSTRATION 32**) established their community on the northwest shores of the Dead Sea. They despised those who controlled the Jerusalem Temple, and looked on themselves as the true Temple and the true messianic community preparing the way in the wilderness for the coming Messiah. Prior to their destruction by the Romans in A.D. 68, they hid their scrolls (the Dead Sea Scrolls) in jars which they stored in caves in the vicinity of their Qumran community.

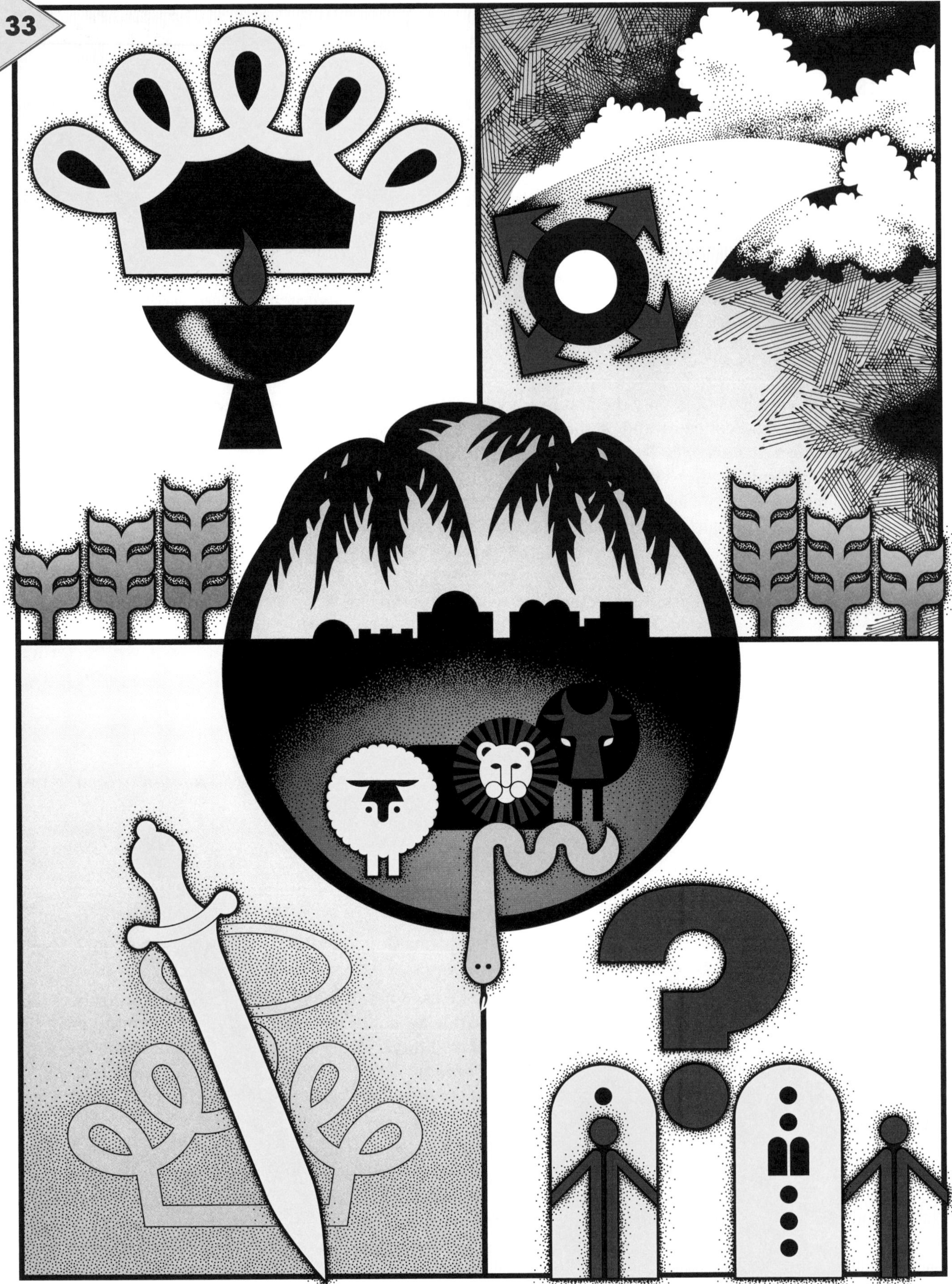
ILLUSTRATION
33

MESSIANIC HOPES

In Jesus' day, the Jews were anxiously waiting for the Messianic Age to break into history.

Center

The Messianic Age

- When the Messianic Age broke in, a beautified Jerusalem (***skyline***) would be at center stage, Isaiah 2:2–4, Micah 4:1–4.
- The land of Israel would become like a new Garden of Eden (***trees over skyline***), Isaiah 51: 1–3; Ezekiel 36:35.
- Even the animals (***lamb***, ***lion***, ***ox***, ***serpent***) would live together in peace, just as they had in the garden of Eden prior to the fall into sin, Isaiah 11:6–9. (Mark 1:13 refers to Jesus being with the wild beasts after His temptation, Mark 1:13; Paradise was being restored, and Satan overthrown.)
- The land would become incredibly fertile (***plants*** *to left and right of center section*). Crops would produce so abundantly that the person plowing the ground in preparation for the next seeding would overtake persons still harvesting the previous crop, Amos 9:13a. Vines would produce grapes in such abundance that the hills would flow with wine, Amos 9:13b.

Upper left, upper right, lower left

The Messianic Deliverer

A number of views prevailed.

- *Upper left:* The Messiah would be a wise (***lamp***), righteous, God-fearing king (***crown***) who would study and obey God's laws, and teach others to do the same, Isaiah 11:1–5.
- *Upper right:* Some hoped that ***God Himself would break in from the heavens*** to rescue His people from the oppressive might of surrounding nations, Isaiah 64:1,2.
- *Lower left:* The Psalms of Solomon 17 and 18 (written by the Pharisees about 50 B.C.) speak of a divine warrior-king (***halo***, ***sword***, ***crown***) who would come with supernatural power to conquer the Gentile nations once and for all. The wealth of the Gentile nations would be brought to Jerusalem in ships across the sea and by camels across the deserts, Isaiah 60:1–61:6.

Lower right section

Participants in the Messianic Age

- All Jews (***those within the covenant***) would take part in the Messianic Age. Naturally, many Jews waited with fanatical fervor for the coming of the Messiah!
- What about the Gentiles—***those outside the covenant***? Some thought that just before the Messiah came, the Gentiles would make one final, desperate attempt to crush God's people—only to be destroyed, Ezekiel 38,39. Some believed that even the "alien" Gentiles would take part in the Messianic Age (Ezekiel 47:21–23) and worship at the Jerusalem Temple, Isaiah 56:6–8. Some believed that when the Messianic Age came, the Gentiles would serve the Jews in a variety of ways, Isaiah 60:10–16, 61:5.

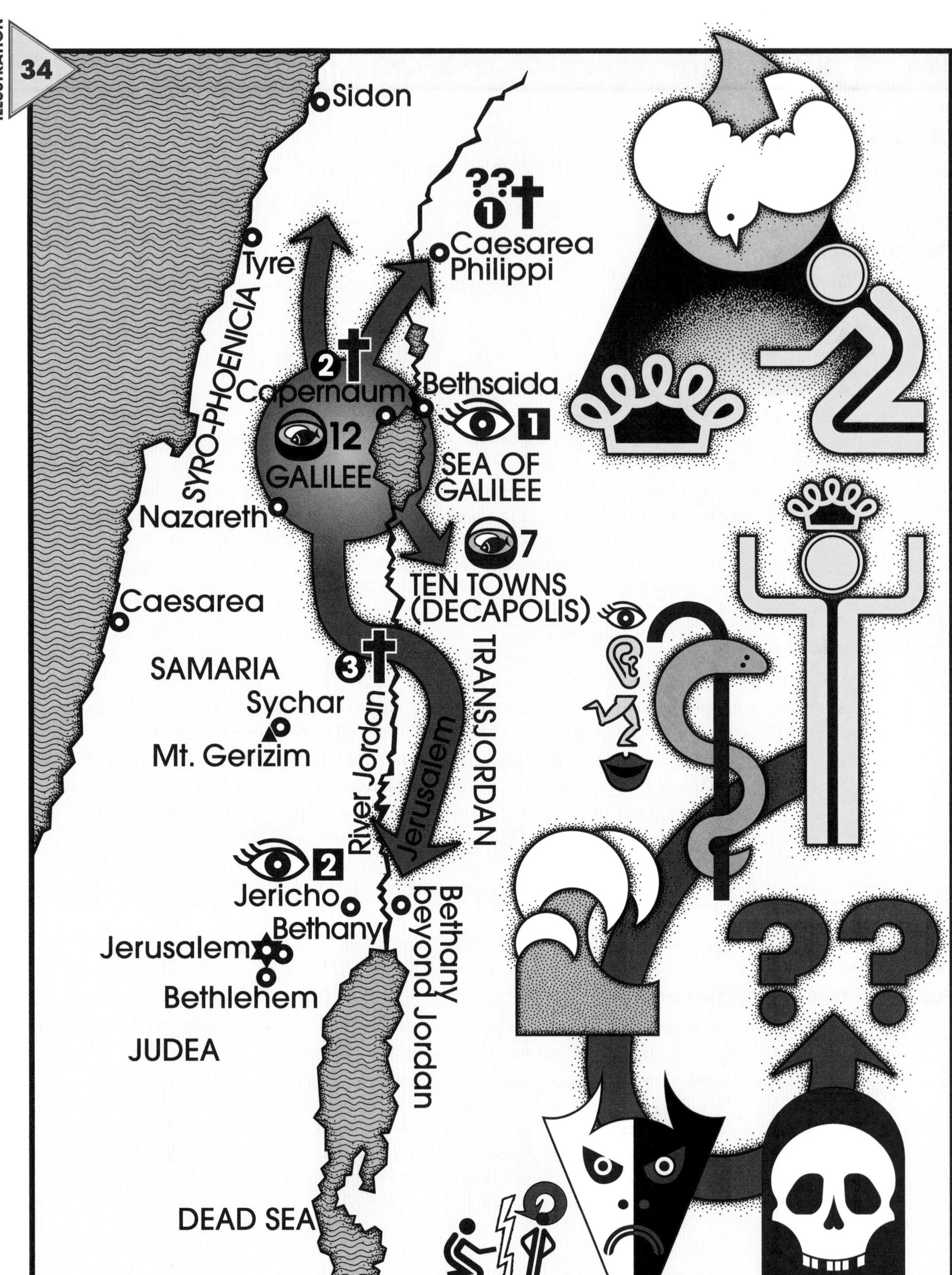
ILLUSTRATION
34
Sidon
Tyre
Caesarea
Philippi
SYRO-PHOENICIA
Capernaum
Bethsaida
12
GALILEE
SEA OF
GALILEE
Nazareth
7
TEN TOWNS
(DECAPOLIS)
Caesarea
SAMARIA
Sychar
Mt. Gerizim
River Jordan
Jerusalem
TRANSJORDAN
Jericho
Bethany
Bethany
beyond Jordan
Jerusalem
Bethlehem
JUDEA
DEAD SEA

The Kingdom of God is at Hand! The Claim 34

Mark begins his Gospel by referring to Jesus as "the Christ," "the Messiah,"1:1. The implication is, "The **Messianic Age** is breaking into history." The question then is: **"What is it like?"**

Mark 1:2 draws on Malachi 3:1 to state that, in Jesus, God will visit His Temple; note Mark 11:11. Mark 1:3 refers to Isaiah 40:3–5 to point out that God is now completing the final rescue, the "final exodus," of His people. The real enemy is not Rome. It is Satan, sin, and death!

When John the Baptist carries out his ministry (at ***Bethany beyond the Jordan***, **ILLUSTRATION 34**, according to John 1:28), Jews come to him for baptism, Mark 1:4–8. This is remarkable, for Jews baptized Gentiles converting to Judaism, but were never baptized themselves.

Jesus comes to John to be baptized (***drop of water***, ***dove***) and to identify with the new movement. Eventually He will lead it. In His baptism (1:9–11), Jesus is declared *King* (***crown***, Psalm 2:7; Psalm 2 is a royal coronation psalm) and *servant* (***servant figure with halo***, Isaiah 42:1; Isaiah 42:1–6 is a "servant song"). Jesus then goes into the wilderness to do battle with ***Satan*** (*bottom right*), the "occupying power," 1:12,13. The key issue is, "Will Jesus walk the way of a servant of others, without limit?" Jesus the Servant is finally "enthroned" at Calvary, vindicated in His resurrection, and declared Lord over the trio of Satan, sin, and death.

During His ministry, Jesus travels south from ***Nazareth*** for His baptism (1:9–11), into the wilderness for the temptation (1:12,13), and then returns to Nazareth, 1:14. He conducts His ministry in ***Galilee*** (1:15–7:23), in ***Syrophoenicia*** (7:24–30), in the ***Decapolis*** (7:31–8:13), and then in ***Bethsaida***, and as far north as ***Caesarea Philippi*** (8:13,22,27). When He feeds 5,000 men in ***Galilee*** *with bread and fish, there are* ***12 baskets*** *of leftovers*—one for each tribe in Israel, 6:30–44. After feeding 4,000 Gentiles in the ***Decapolis*** (8:1–10), there are ***seven baskets*** *of leftovers*. (The Jewish people often expressed hatred for the seven nations living on their borders; see Deut. 7:1–7). Jesus finally enters ***Jerusalem*** five days before His crucifixion, 11:1.

Although Mark states that Jesus *teaches*, he reports little about what Jesus *says*. However, Jesus' whole *life* proclaims, "I am a King who walks the way of a Servant." Jesus' life demonstrates the Kingdom He came to establish and the life to which He summons people. Though Jesus does not declare in *words* that He is God or Messiah, His *actions* do. The miracles reported in Mark's first eight chapters can be divided into four groups (see **ILLUSTRATION 34**, *lower right*):

a. ***Miracles over sickness*** (***serpent around staff;*** see Numbers 21:4–9)***:*** Jesus gives sight to the *blind* (***eye***), hearing to the *deaf* (***ear***), healthy bodies to the *crippled* (***legs***), speech to the *dumb* (***mouth***)—thus fulfilling Isaiah's "signs" (Isaiah 35:5,6). He heals two blind men, one at Bethsaida (***eye 1***, 8:22–26), another at Jericho (***eye 2***, 10:46–52).

b. ***Miracles over nature*** (***white-capped waves***)***:*** Jesus demonstrates power over "the deep," 4:35–41, 6:45–52. The Psalms ascribed this same power to God; see 89:9; 107:23–32.

c. ***Miracles over demons*** (***demonic face***)***:*** Jesus casts out many demons and commands them to be silent about His identity, 1:23, 32, 34, 39; 5:2; 7:25; see also 3:22–27. Satan's goal was and remains, *"Don't serve God and others! Serve yourself!"*

d. ***Miracles over death*** (***tombstone***)***:*** Jesus raises the dead (Mark 5:21–24, 35–43), thus fulfilling the "messianic hope" expressed in Isaiah 25:8, 26:19 and Daniel 12:2.

After doing the miracles outlined in 5 above, Jesus, on the way to Caesarea Philippi, asks the disciples ***two questions***: "Who do *the people* think I am?" "Who do *you* think I am?" Peter answers that though *the people* do not see Him as the Messiah, *the disciples* do, 8:27–30. When Jesus then predicts His coming passion three times (***crosses 1***, ***2*** and ***3***), the disciples never understand!

ILLUSTRATION
35
TRANSFIGURATION
TO JERUSALEM

The Kingdom of God is at Hand! The Verdict 35

Upper Section

Though the disciples recognize Jesus to be the Messiah, they do not understand what kind of a Messiah He is, and what being involved with Jesus implies for them. Their eyes have not been fully opened to "see" the truth concerning Jesus' identity and mission, Mark 8:22–26; 10:46–52 (***eye 1*** and ***eye 2*** in **ILLUSTRATION 34** and **ILLUSTRATION 35**). This is made clear in the following cycles of events:

- ***Prediction:*** Jesus predicts His approaching passion three times, 8:31; 9:30–32;10:32–34 (***crosses 1***, ***2*** and ***3***). Each prediction follows a significant event—the *first* after Peter's confession at Caesarea Philippi, 8:27–30; the *second* after Jesus' Transfiguration (9:2–8); the *third* after Jesus leaves Galilee to go to Jerusalem—and death by crucifixion, 10:1,32.
- ***Confusion:*** Each time Jesus predicts His passion, the disciples' confused responses reveal that their goal is power, position, prestige, and prominence, 8:32; 9:33,34; 10:35–37. Jesus' teachings about ***servanthood*** and ***carrying the cross*** confuse them.
- ***Clarification:*** Jesus responds to the disciples' confusion by stressing that involvement with Him implies servanthood without limit, 8:33–38; 9:35; 10:41–45.

Middle Section

Jesus enters Jerusalem on the Sunday prior to Passover, 11:1–10. By entering on a donkey, He asserts that He comes on a mission of peace, Zechariah 9:9. The first thing He does is to examine the Temple, Judaism's holiest place, Mark 11:11; note Malachi 3:1. The next day Jesus causes chaos in the Temple, 11:15–19. He attacks those in charge for denying Gentiles access to the Temple, and for exploiting worshipers through the sacrificial system, 11:17; see Isaiah 56:7; Jeremiah 7:11.

Jerusalem's political and religious leaders now confront Jesus with a demand that He justify His actions. Jesus responds by putting them in a dilemma (11:27–33) and by assuring them that unless they mend their ways swiftly and radically, His Father will take the Kingdom from them and give it to the Gentiles, 12:1–12. The authorities are furious!

In quick succession, Jesus handles ***questions*** put to Him by the *Pharisees and Herodians* (12:13–17; ***coin***); the *Sadducees* (12:18–27; ***divided grave***) and a *scribe* (12:28–34; ***law-code***). Jesus then points out that though they are expecting David's son, the One who has come is a much bigger Son than they realize! Jesus is not merely David's physical descendant, "lord"; He is David's *Lord and God* (12:35–37; ***crown***).

Lower Section

Only the faithful remnant, those who acknowledge Jesus as their Messiah, Savior and Lord, belong to God's True Israel. Though Jesus comes as ***the new and true Israel***, few understand Him and most reject Him. They fail to *see* that His actions point to the breaking in of the Messianic Kingdom, and His manner of life to its true nature (***Servant King***). (The ***four question marks*** refer to Jesus' words and actions depicted in **ILLUSTRATION 34**, *lower right*—miracles over sickness, nature, demons, and death.) During Holy Week, it appears Jesus' mission will crumble. The disciples desert Jesus and the authorities crucify Him (***cross***). However, God vindicates and endorses Jesus by raising Him from the dead (***open tomb***).

The disciples and some of the people will begin to *see* when they meet the Risen Lord in Galilee, 16:1–8; note ***eye 3*** and "see," v. 7. **Those who "see," who finally come to faith in Jesus as Messiah, Savior and Lord, become the nucleus of the new community that will proclaim the risen and ascended Jesus (*rising arrow*) to the world! The Holy Spirit (*dove*) equips and empowers them for their ministry to the world.**

ILLUSTRATION 36

The Nature of the Messianic Kingdom

 Some people believe that the Old Testament people of God were to save themselves by obedience to the commandments given at Sinai. This is not true. Salvation has always been *by grace, through faith* in God's merciful forgiveness of sins—a faith that expresses itself in obedience. The word *grace* weaves its way all through the Old Testament.

 It is true that, during the period between the Testaments, some within Judaism thought that salvation was *by works*. They viewed the commandments as a *merit system* rather than as a *response system*.

 The issue at stake in the Gospels is: What kind of a Messiah was Jesus? What was the nature of Jesus' Kingship? What kind of kingdom did He establish? Though the Jews were waiting for a Messiah, they were not expecting the life-style of the Messiah to be that of a servant.

 **ILLUSTRATION 36** draws on John 13:1–17 to portray the nature of Jesus' Messiahship. It shows ***Jesus on His knees washing Peter's feet***.

- As **ILLUSTRATION 34** depicted, at His baptism, Jesus was declared to be ***King*** ("You are my Son, the Beloved," Mark 1:11; see Psalm 2:7; Psalm 2 is a royal coronation psalm) and ***Servant*** ("with You I am well pleased," Mark 1:11; see Isaiah 42:1; Isaiah 42:1–6 is a "servant psalm"). Symbols pointing to these truths are at the *center* of **ILLUSTRATION 36** (***Servant King***).
- Also included are symbols of Jesus' crucifixion and resurrection (***cross*** and ***open tomb***). When Jesus went to the cross, He went there as **the Servant without limit**. None who witnessed Jesus' trial and crucifixion expected Jesus to return to life. However, Jesus' Father raised Him from the dead and, in so doing, gave **the casting vote that declared Jesus to be the Messiah!**
- Around the symbols depicting Jesus' ministry is a ***circle of people holding hands in community***. God's desire is that all live in community, seeking to glorify God and serve each other in all they do. Unlike most humans, God is not interested in national borders, flags, and skin colors.

 God sends the Holy Spirit (***dove***) to help people understand, believe, and embrace the tremendous truths that relate to Jesus' ministry, and to empower them to live as members of Jesus' servant community. As **ILLUSTRATION 38** will point out, the Holy Spirit uses the Holy Scriptures, baptism, and the Lord's Supper to communicate God's truth to humanity, to bring them to faith in Jesus as Savior and Lord, and to empower them to walk in the way of discipleship in servant community.

ILLUSTRATION 37

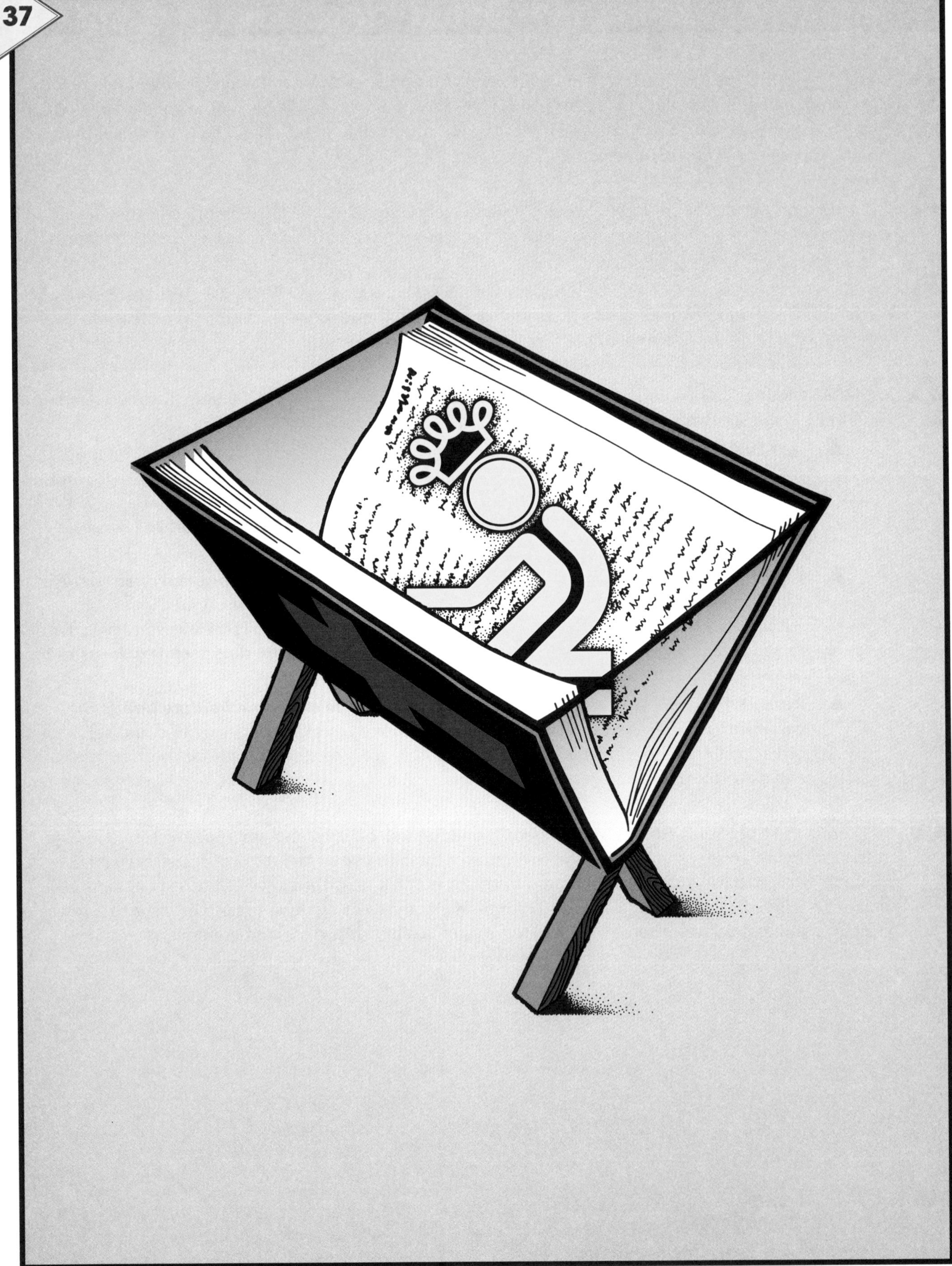

The Word Made Flesh

ILLUSTRATION 37 depicts in graphic form Martin Luther's statement, "The Bible is the cradle which brings us Jesus of Nazareth." New Testament writings support and amplify this insight.

The Word in Judaism

 The rabbis, or Jewish teachers, of Jesus' day taught that the first thing God created was the *Torah*, the Pentateuch, the first five books of Moses. They said that though the Torah was created before the universe, God eventually dictated it to Moses at Sinai. They also said that though other books in the Jewish Scriptures were inspired, they were not transmitted through dictation from God.

 Some rabbis equated the Torah with *Wisdom*, eventually personified Wisdom, and said that Wisdom was not only the blueprint on which creation was based, but the very architect of creation; see Proverbs 8:23, 27. Some identified Wisdom with the written Law, and insisted that Wisdom dwelt only in Israel, Sirach 24:3,4.

 Rabbis generally referred to the Torah as *the bread of life*, *the water of life*, and *the light of the world.*

The Word in the New Testament

 The New Testament teaches that, in Jesus, the Word of God became a Person, John 1:14. God's "final word" to humanity is seen and heard in Jesus, Hebrews 1:1–4.

 Matthew teaches that in Jesus:

- One greater than the *Temple* has come, 12:6.
- One greater than the *Sabbath* has come, 12:7. (The observance of the Sabbath receives much attention in Exodus 20:8–11 and Deuteronomy 5:12–15.)
- One greater than *Jonah* has come, 12:41. (Jonah was sent to preach to the Gentiles.)
- One greater than *Solomon* has come, 12:42. (Compare Matthew 2:11 with 1 Kings 10:23–25. Note 1 Corinthians 1:24.)

These pronouncements would have greatly angered Jesus' hearers.

 John speaks of Jesus as:

- The bread of life, 6:41;
- The water of life, 4:7–15;
- The light of the world, 8:12, 9:5.

In short, the written Word points beyond itself to the Living Word, Jesus the Messiah.

38

38

The Word Made Flesh

ILLUSTRATION 37 depicts in graphic form Martin Luther's statement, "The Bible is the cradle which brings us Jesus of Nazareth." New Testament writings support and amplify this insight.

The Word in Judaism

 The rabbis, or Jewish teachers, of Jesus' day taught that the first thing God created was the *Torah*, the Pentateuch, the first five books of Moses. They said that though the Torah was created before the universe, God eventually dictated it to Moses at Sinai. They also said that though other books in the Jewish Scriptures were inspired, they were not transmitted through dictation from God.

 Some rabbis equated the Torah with *Wisdom*, eventually personified Wisdom, and said that Wisdom was not only the blueprint on which creation was based, but the very architect of creation; see Proverbs 8:23, 27. Some identified Wisdom with the written Law, and insisted that Wisdom dwelt only in Israel, Sirach 24:3,4.

 Rabbis generally referred to the Torah as *the bread of life*, *the water of life*, and *the light of the world.*

The Word in the New Testament

 The New Testament teaches that, in Jesus, the Word of God became a Person, John 1:14. God's "final word" to humanity is seen and heard in Jesus, Hebrews 1:1–4.

 Matthew teaches that in Jesus:

- One greater than the *Temple* has come, 12:6.
- One greater than the *Sabbath* has come, 12:7. (The observance of the Sabbath receives much attention in Exodus 20:8–11 and Deuteronomy 5:12–15.)
- One greater than *Jonah* has come, 12:41. (Jonah was sent to preach to the Gentiles.)
- One greater than *Solomon* has come, 12:42. (Compare Matthew 2:11 with 1 Kings 10:23–25. Note 1 Corinthians 1:24.)

These pronouncements would have greatly angered Jesus' hearers.

 John speaks of Jesus as:

- The bread of life, 6:41;
- The water of life, 4:7–15;
- The light of the world, 8:12, 9:5.

In short, the written Word points beyond itself to the Living Word, Jesus the Messiah.

Jesus and the Spirit

 God united His deity with humanity when Mary conceived, Luke 1:31. The God-Man, Jesus the Messiah, lived the life of a ***sinless Servant***, was ***crucified***, ***died***, and ***was buried*** (**ILLUSTRATION 38**, *center left*). Jesus showed His glory in a strange way—by walking the way of a humble Servant-without-limit.

 On Easter Sunday morning, ***Jesus rose from the dead***. He left the tomb before the stone was rolled away. The stone was rolled away, not to let Jesus out, but to let people in.

 Jesus' post-resurrection appearances to His disciples and others were *little visits* to let them know that He was still among them—though in a transformed manner.

 When Jesus ***ascended*** (***arrow rising from open tomb into cloud***), He did not *withdraw* His presence; He *transformed* it. In rising from the ground, Jesus was saying to His disciples, "No more little visible visits—until I finally reappear at the end of the age. Even so, I will remain with you until the end of the age," Matthew 28:20; Luke 24:50–53. In the ascension narrative recorded in Acts 1:1–11, Jesus made it clear to His still-confused disciples that He had no intention of reestablishing an earthly, political Davidic kingdom!

 Though Jesus said that after He ascended He would send the Holy Spirit to His disciples (John 14:26; 16:7), He also said that He Himself would come and abide with them (John 14:18), and that He and the Father would come and make their home with the disciples, John 14:23.

 The triumphant, ascended Jesus *returns* (or better, "*remains*"; ***descending arrow***) and continues His work through the Holy Spirit (***dove***) who speaks to humanity through the Holy Scriptures, Baptism and Holy Communion (***Bible***, ***drop of water***, ***bread and cup***, *bottom right*).

 Jesus summons His followers to *reflect His glory* during their lives (*servanthood*), and promises that He will finally take them to *share His glory* in the presence of the Father, John 17:22–24 (***arrow at right goes up into cloud***).

When those taken into exile in Babylon in 597 and 587 B.C. began returning to Judah in 538 B.C., they faced a dilemma. In Babylon, the exiles had adopted Aramaic as their language. However, their scriptures were written in Hebrew, had to be read in Hebrew, and rabbis had to preach in Hebrew. To solve this language problem, rabbis made use of an interpreter (*methurgeman* in Aramaic). The interpreter listened carefully to what the rabbi read and proclaimed—and translated it into Aramaic so that the worshipers could understand it. This sheds light on Jesus' words in John 14:26 (see also 16:14):

> *But the Advocate, the Holy Spirit, whom the Father will send in My name, will teach you everything, and will remind you of all that I have said to you.* (John 14:26; see also 16:14)

We do not need to ask the Holy Spirit to "come." The Holy Spirit is always present. But because the Holy Spirit teaches people about Jesus through the Scriptures, it is essential that people read, study, and listen to those Scriptures—and listen to the Spirit's voice as it speaks and teaches through them.

Exodus 3 and Creation 3

ILLUSTRATION 39 uses and develops truths depicted in **ILLUSTRATIONS 5**, **10**, and **25**.

Upper section

Creation 1 and ***Exodus 1***

ILLUSTRATION 5 depicted God's role as the creator and owner of heaven and earth (***Creation 1***). **ILLUSTRATION 10** depicted the first Exodus, in which God rescued His people from bondage in Egypt (***Exodus 1***).

Middle section

Creation 2 and ***Exodus 2***

ILLUSTRATION 25 depicted how the concepts of *exodus* and *creation* are used to describe God's rescue of His people from bondage in Babylon.

Lower section

Exodus 3 and ***Creation 3***

ILLUSTRATION 39 shows how the New Testament draws on this terminology to go one step further in presenting Jesus' mission as *the final exodus* (or *rescue*) *event* that brings about the *new creation*. (Note: The word in Luke 9:31 translated as *departure* (NRSV) is actually *exodus* in the original Greek.)

Exodus 3

All four Gospels quote Isaiah 40:3 when introducing John the Baptist and Jesus, Mark 1:3 and parallel passages; John 1:23. Through His ***servant life***, ***death***, ***burial***, and ***resurrection***, Jesus the ***Servant King*** rescues us from bondage (***chains***) to ***Satan***, ***sin***, ***law***, and ***death***. He adopts us into His community (Galatians 4:4,5; Ephesians 1:5,6) through the *water-crossing of baptism* (***drop of water on arrow leading from chains to Jesus***).

Creation 3

Through Jesus' work, God produces a "new creation" (***hand***, *top right*) within the ***human heart***. God "re-creates" a person from a *servant of self* to a *servant of God through the service of others*. (Note: "In the beginning," John 1:1, Genesis 1:1; "He has done everything well," Mark 7:37, Genesis 1:31; "So, if anyone is in Christ, there is *a new creation*," 2 Corinthians 5:17.)

There is nothing wrong with laws and commandments. The problem is that people see obedience to laws and commandments as a "merit system" that will earn them salvation. Therefore, they tend to do the *right thing* for the *wrong reason*.

It is important to understand that obedience to commandments does not *affect*, or bring about, salvation. It merely *reflects* salvation in terms of faith in Jesus the Messiah. Furthermore, the pattern of behavior that Christians are to pursue is not a collection of laws, but is the life of Jesus, their ***Servant King***.

Making Visible the Invisible Jesus

1 The explanatory notes for **ILLUSTRATION 37** referred to Martin Luther's comment, "The Bible is the cradle that brings us Jesus of Nazareth." This truth is reflected in **ILLUSTRATION 40** where the figure of Jesus, the ***Servant King***, is superimposed upon a symbol for the ***Bible***. The Jesus revealed in the Bible is still with and among us—forgiving, serving, guiding, and empowering us.

Jesus does not ask us to put Him *first*—but *only*. The word *first* quoted in Matthew 6:33 does not occur in the parallel passage in Luke 12:31. Furthermore, in Matthew 4:10 Jesus says we are to worship God and serve Him *only*.

The Christian faith is not the most important *part of life*; it is *life itself*. Christians see all of life as a sacred affair, lived in the presence of Jesus. Their one desire is to reflect Jesus' servant mind and manner in all they think, say, and do.

- ***Dome:*** Christians live as informed and responsible citizens, helping to empower all to live together harmoniously at local, national, and international levels.
- ***Diplomas:*** Christians develop their skills and abilities to be equipped to serve others in meaningful, useful ways—in their work, studies, homes, etc.
- ***Plate, knife, and fork:*** Christians eat healthfully in order to live usefully. They eat to live; they do not live to eat.
- ***Family:*** The family is the basic unit of society. Parents influence their children enormously, whether they realize it or not. The Christian faith must be taught, first and foremost, in the family circle by parents who equip themselves to know, share, and model the truths they embrace.
- ***Dollar sign:*** Money is servanthood in a storable, transferable form. It is not wrong to have money. The question is: How did we get it and how are we using it?
- ***Ball:*** People need to participate in leisure activities and intellectual pursuits so as to keep their bodies healthy and their minds alert.
- ***Factory:*** Christians see daily work as a service opportunity to do useful things or produce needed products for the good of humanity.
- ***Church building:*** According to the Bible, *church* is always a community of people—never a building. Nevertheless, Christians gather with other Christians in an "ecclesiastical facility" to worship God together and to help one another grow in faith and discipleship.

ILLUSTRATION 41

POWER
POSITION
PROFIT
PLEASURE

Beware of the Enemy!

C.S. Lewis once wrote, "There is no neutral ground in the universe. Every square inch is claimed by God and counterclaimed by Satan." The Bible, in particular the New Testament, teaches us that two kingdoms or realms seek to control our lives.

Upper section

The Kingdom of God

The Kingdom of God does not have geographical borders or political frontiers. It consists of people who live in faith and ***servanthood*** under ***God*** as their gracious, forgiving ***King***. They live to serve God and others.

The Holy Spirit (***dove***) uses the ***Bible's message*** to reveal to us God's truth about ***Jesus, the Messiah—crucified, but risen and present***.

Through Holy Baptism (***drop of water***; Romans 6:1–4), God adopts people in forgiving grace (***cross***) into his family. God's baptized people do not strive to *become* God's people. Their desire is to *show that they are God's people* and *Jesus' brothers and sisters*.

When God's people celebrate Holy Communion, the Lord's Supper, or the Eucharist (***bread and cup***), they celebrate belonging to God's forgiven family, being brothers and sisters of Jesus. They also share their desire to live in servant community, seeking to make visible the invisible Jesus whom they receive through the bread and wine of the sacrament, 1 Corinthians 11:23–26. After eating what they are, they go forth to become what they eat.

Lower section

The Kingdom of the Devil, the World, and our Flesh

The Bible frequently refers to Satan, 1 Chronicles 21:1; Matthew 4:1–11; 1 Peter 5:8,9; Revelation 12:9 (***demonic face***, *top left*). The "satanic" is every spirit, institution, power, or pressure that would sidetrack us from living to serve God and others into serving ourselves.

Satan's "behavior code" for the world, for humanity, is: "Forget all that 'God stuff.' All that matters is ***power*** *for self*, ***position*** *for self*, ***profit*** *for self*, and ***pleasure*** *for self*."

Satan works through a fallen world and the ***sinful human heart*** (*bottom center*) to persuade people to live for themselves—which is really for Satan. Satan is quite happy to have people live decent lives as the world judges decency—as long as they think their "good deeds" make them acceptable to God.

Those who live under the *deadly trio* (described in 1, 2, and 3 above) reject God as King of their lives and adopt an ***indifferent or arrogant posture toward God*** (*bottom right*).

Both of these Kingdoms struggle for control of the lives of Christians, Ephesians 6:10–18. The Kingdom of God is present only *imperfectly* in Christians in this life; it will be present *perfectly* only in the life to come.

In times of prosperity and ease, we should reflect on a statement made by Juvenal, a Roman satirist of the first century A.D., "Luxury is more ruthless than war!"

ILLUSTRATION 42

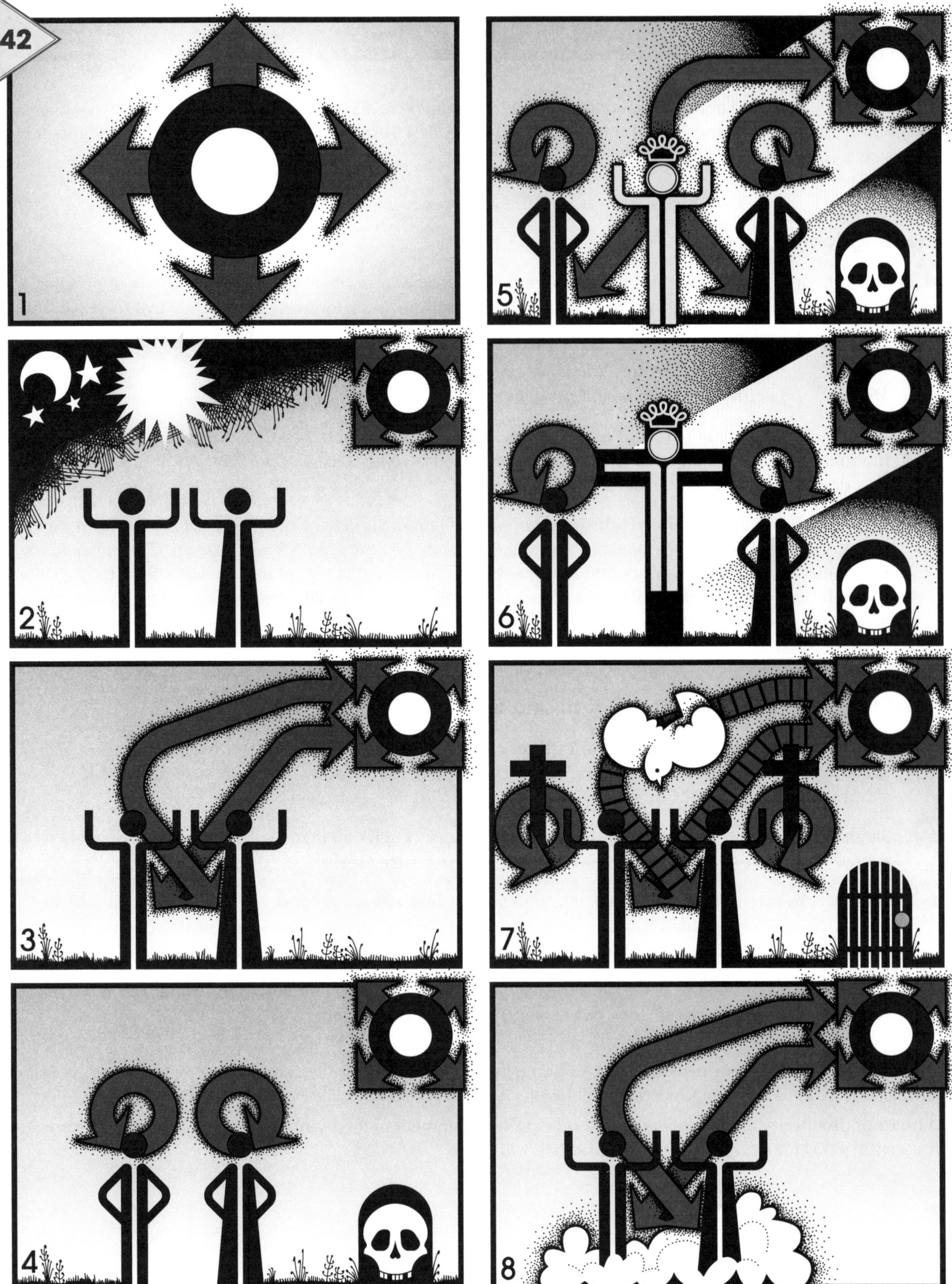

The Sweep of the Divine Plan

The points listed below relate to the eight frames in **ILLUSTRATION 42**.

 1 "In the beginning, God…" Genesis 1:1 (***symbol for God***).

 2 "… created the heavens and the earth," Genesis 1:1 (***sun, moon and stars***; ***surface of earth***). "Then God said, 'Let us make humankind,'" Genesis 1:26. "Male and female He created them," Genesis 1:27 (***male and female figures***).

 3 "…in our image, according to our likeness," Genesis 1:26. People serve God and one another with outgoing love (***double-pointed arrows***).

 4 Humanity sinned. People now live to serve themselves (***circular arrows***). Death is the consequence (***tombstone and skull***), Romans 5:12; 6:23.

 5 People changed; God did not. He became the God-Man in Jesus the Messiah, and lived the life we were meant to live (see also ***frame 3***), but cannot. Jesus lived to serve His Father and others—full-time and without limit.

 6 Jesus suffered the death we deserve to die (***cross***) as punishment for our sins. Jesus' crucifixion was also His coronation (***crown above cross***), because when His opponents did their worst to Him, He did His best for them and us—as the *Servant without limit*. Pilate's superscription, "the King of the Jews" (John 19:19), although meant to be a taunt, expressed a sublime truth.

 7 Jesus lived a sinless life for us, died to suffer our punishment, and rose again from the grave as Lord of life, death, and eternity. He is among us through His Spirit (***dove***) to assure us that our sins are forgiven (***cross through sin***), and that death has been transformed from a fearsome event into a doorway leading to His Eternal Home (***door with slats***; we can see in faith what lies on the other side of death). God now desires that we strive to live according to His original plan—depicted in **ILLUSTRATION 6** (***arrows to God and neighbor***; ***broken, because our obedience is at best imperfect***).

 8 In the life to come (***the cloud symbolizing God's presence***), God will restore all things so that they conform to His original plan. In eternity we shall live to praise God and serve others. While we wait for Jesus to welcome us into His Eternal Home, we are to heed His one commandment (John 13:34,35) and serve God *full-time* by serving others *full-time*, Matthew 25:31–46.

ILLUSTRATION
43

The Goal of the Divine Plan

 **ILLUSTRATION 6** depicted God's original plan.

 **ILLUSTRATION 7** depicted what happened to that plan when the power of sin broke into the human scene.

 The goal of Jesus' ministry (outlined in **ILLUSTRATIONS 34** through **42**) was, and is, to restore God's plan in time and for eternity. **ILLUSTRATION 43** shows that plan restored in Christ.

 In Ephesians 1:9,10 (RSV), Paul writes:

> *God has made known to us in all wisdom and insight the mystery of his will, according to his purpose which he set forth in Christ, as a plan for the fulness of time,* ***to unite all things in Him, things in heaven and things on earth.***

The Anglican Catechism asks: "What is the mission of the Church?" and answers:

> *The mission of the Church is to restore all people to unity with God and each other, in Christ.*

Scholars and teachers in the Church have expressed the mission of the Church as follows:

> *The Church is called to be a provisional display of God's original intention.* (Karl Barth)
>
> *The mission of the Church in time is to work for the restoration of cosmic unity.* (Martin Scharlemann)

These statements challenge the notion that Christianity is merely a "next world" faith. Though Christianity does point people to the sure hope of life after death, it calls Christians to learn to live *now* as they will *then*—as full-time servants of God and each other.

 If all people on earth asked, "How can I use life to glorify God by serving those around me—regardless of borders, flags, and skin color—in the spirit of Jesus?" life on earth would be totally different.

 A Chinese proverb states: "When a butterfly flaps its wings in China, it affects the weather patterns around the planet." The message of this proverb reflects Jesus' teaching and calls us as His followers to ask:

> If everyone on earth were to live as I choose to live and to pursue the life-style that I elect to follow, what would life be like on this little planet? If the "ripple effect" of others adopting and pursuing my way of life results in harm to, and neglect of, creation and others, I have no right to live that way or pursue that life-style.

 It follows that there is no such thing as private or secret Christianity. Christians are called to *personal* faith, but never *private* faith. Christians are called not merely to *believe* in Jesus, but also to *follow* Him—to live as servants of God and others in community.

ILLUSTRATION
44

The Grand Finale to the Divine Plan

ILLUSTRATION 44 consists of three sections which are explained below, incorporating these four points.

 The Gospels stress the importance of taking seriously the final appearance of Jesus at the end of time, e.g. Matthew chs. 24,25. (All passages referred to below are from Matthew's Gospel.)

 Jesus predicted the destruction of the Jewish nation and of the Jerusalem Temple by the Romans, 24: 1,2; 24:15–28. These predictions came to pass in A.D. 66–70. In 24:3–14, Jesus speaks of troubles that will occur in the religious and political realms prior to His final appearing, 24:29–31.

 In several parables, Jesus stresses that the faithful must be ready at all times for His final appearing. He encourages the faithful and warns the lax, 24:45–51. When He reappears, some will be ready and some will be caught unprepared, 25:1–13; therefore, *live expectantly!* The faithful are to use their abilities and possessions in a God-pleasing manner while waiting for the final day, 25:14–30; therefore, *live responsibly!* Finally, in 25:31–46 Jesus appeals to His followers to *live compassionately*.

 While waiting for Jesus' final appearance, Jesus' followers are to confess Him before the world (10: 32,33), demonstrate a discipleship that reflects Jesus (10:7,8), baptize in the name of the Triune God (28:19,20), and teach and exhort others to do God's will—remembering at all times that they are members of an eternal community in whose midst Jesus dwells, 28:20. When the end finally comes, the Lord will reveal His presence in glory and splendor to welcome into His Father's eternal home those who have believed in and followed Him, 25:34.

Upper section

In Matthew 25:31–46, Jesus describes the final day of history:

- Jesus will return in glory (***crowned, triumphant Jesus in posture of welcome***), command all graves to give up their dead, and gather all nations before Him, v. 31.
- Jesus will then separate humanity into two groups, placing the ***sheep*** at His right hand and the ***goats*** at His left hand, vv. 32,33.
- Jesus will speak first to the sheep at His right. He will address words of invitation ("Come") to those who are blessed by His Father (v. 34), and invite them to inherit the kingdom prepared for them from the foundation of the world.
- Those finally received into the Father's house are welcomed ("Come", 25:34) solely because they are "blessed" by Jesus' Father. They "inherit" (not "merit") the "kingdom" prepared "*for* them" (not "*by* them") before the beginning of time (when they were not present to help prepare it), Matthew 25:31–34. Boasting is out; grace reigns supreme!

Middle section

- Jesus will graciously commend those He welcomes for acts of service done to others (***servant figures***). They gave ***food*** to the hungry, ***drink*** to the thirsty, ***companionship to the lonely***, and ***clothing*** to those lacking it. They also visited and cared for the *sick* (***symbol of healing, serpent around staff***; see Numbers 21:4–9), and visited the ***prisoner***. In serving people in these situations of need, they were really serving Jesus "in distressing disguise"—a term used by Mother Theresa.
- Jesus will reject those who claim to know Him as "Lord" (Matthew 25:44), but have never followed Him in servant discipleship. Jesus does not refer to any evil that they might have done, but to the good they failed to do. They failed to see Jesus all around them in distressing disguise.

- Matthew 25:31–46 reminds us that we must distinguish between *the basis of acceptance* (God's grace), and *the basis of commendation* (service rendered to others, and so to God). Christians do not perform deeds of service for the sake of reward, but to meet other people's needs, Matthew 25:37–39. Their desire is to reflect Jesus in all they do.

Lower section

- ***Food and drink*** *(left)***:** The Gospels frequently refer to Jesus sharing a meal with His disciples and followers. His followers today need to understand that He is present with them constantly (Matthew 28:20)—and in a very meaningful way at every mealtime. In Jesus' day, those who ate together declared: "We are family! We will serve each other, and defend each other to the death!"
- ***Basin and towel*** *(right)***:** Jesus' followers are to serve each other, even as Jesus served His disciples by washing their feet.
- ***Drop of water—baptism*** *(center)***:** When people are baptized, they are adopted into God's family and God shares His Son's sinless life, death, burial, and resurrection with them, Romans 6:1–14. Jesus says to those adopted into His kingdom in Baptism: "I lived the life you were meant to live—but have not lived and cannot live. I give you My sinless life to possess as your very own; you can look on My life as though you yourself lived it. You went to the cross with Me—and because I shared My cross with you, you no longer need to suffer any punishment for sin. You went into the tomb with Me, and so have already endured the grave that sin brings. I rose from the dead—and I share My resurrection with you. Eternal life is already yours; you merely wait to join Me in that eternal realm you already possess. So while you wait to join Me in heaven, seek to live the heavenly life already on earth."

  Thus, God's people no longer strive to *become* God's people. Their desire is rather to show that they *are* God's people. They strive to live on earth as they will eventually live in heaven.
- ***Bread and cup*** *(center)***:** Jesus' spiritual brothers and sisters are "remembered" to Him in the Eucharist—that is, linked to Him and His saving work, and to each other. Having celebrated their membership in Jesus' community by eating what they are, they go forth to become what they eat.

  In short, they are to make Jesus visible in all they do by living as His servant-people in community.